THE GREEK ISLANDS
Genius Loci

View of Naxos island seen through the monumental doorway of the Archaic temple.
Thomas Hope (1769-1831)   Watercolour, 44 x 29 cm.   Benaki Museum, Inv. No. 27375.
© 2010 Benaki Museum, Athens.

Author's acknowledgements

This series of twenty books covering the Aegean Islands is the fruit of many years of solitary dedication to a job difficult to accomplish given the extent of the subject matter and the geography involved. My belief throughout has been that only what is seen with the eyes can trustfully be written about; and to that end I have attempted to walk, ride, drive, climb, sail and swim these Islands in order to inspect everything talked about here. There will be errors in this text inevitably for which, although working in good faith, I alone am responsible. Notwithstanding, I am confident that these are the best, most clearly explanatory and most comprehensive artistic accounts currently available of this vibrant and historically dense corner of the Mediterranean.

Professor Robin Barber, author of the last, general, *Blue Guide to Greece* (based in turn on Stuart Rossiter's masterful text of the 1960s), has been very generous with support and help; and I am also particularly indebted to Charles Arnold for meticulously researched factual data on the Islands and for his support throughout this project. I could not have asked for a more saintly and helpful editor, corrector and indexer than Judy Tither. Efi Stathopoulou, Peter Cocconi, Marc René de Montalembert, Valentina Ivancich, William Forrester and Geoffrey Cox have all given invaluable help; and I owe a large debt of gratitude to John and Jay Rendall for serial hospitality and encouragement. For companionship on many journeys, I would like to thank a number of dear friends: Graziella Seferiades, Ivan Tabares, Matthew Kidd, Martin Leon, my group of Louisianan friends, and my brother Iain— all of whose different reactions to and passions for Greece have been a constant inspiration.

This work is dedicated with admiration and deep affection to Ivan de Jesus Tabares-Valencia who, though a native of the distant Andes mountains, from the start understood the profound spiritual appeal of the Aegean world.

McGILCHRIST'S GREEK ISLANDS

8. KYTHERA
WITH ANTIKYTHERA
& ELAFONISOS

GENIUS LOCI PUBLICATIONS
London

McGilchrist's Greek Islands 8. Kythera with Antikythera & Elafonisos
First edition

Published by Genius Loci Publications
54 Eccleston Road, London W13 0RL

Nigel McGilchrist © 2010
Nigel McGilchrist has asserted his moral rights.

ISBN 978-1-907859-09-0

A CIP catalogue record of this book is available from the British Library.

The author and publisher cannot accept responsibility or liability for
information contained herein, this being in some cases difficult to verify
and subject to change.

Layout and copy-editing by Judy Tither

Cover design by Kate Buckle

Maps and plans by Nick Hill Design

Printed and bound in Great Britain by TJ International Ltd, Padstow, Cornwall

The island maps in this series are based on the cartography of
Terrain Maps
Karneadou 4, 106 75 Athens, Greece
T: +30 210 609 5759, Fx: +30 210 609 5859
terrain@terrainmaps.gr
www.terrainmaps.gr

This book is one of twenty which comprise the complete, detailed
manuscript which the author prepared for the *Blue Guide: Greece,
the Aegean Islands* (2010), and on which the *Blue Guide* was
based. Some of this text therefore appears in the *Blue Guide*.

A NOTE ON THE TEXT & MAPS

Some items in the text are marked with an asterisk: these may be monuments, landscapes, curiosities or individual artefacts and works of art. The asterisk is not simply an indication of the renown of a particular place or item, but is intended to draw the reader's attention to things that have a uniquely interesting quality or are of particular beauty.

A small number of hotels and eateries are also marked with asterisks in the *Practical Information* sections, implying that their quality or their setting is notably special. These books do not set out to be guides to lodging and eating in the Islands, and our recommendations here are just an attempt to help with a few suggestions for places that have been selected with an eye to simplicity and unpretentiousness. We believe they may be the kind of places that a reader of this book would be seeking and would enjoy.

On the island maps:

⁘   denotes a site with visible prehistoric or ancient remains

✝   denotes a church referred to in the text
(on Island Maps only rural churches are marked)

✝   denotes a monastery, convent or large church referred to in the text

⌂   denotes a Byzantine or Mediaeval castle

♨   denotes an important fresh-water or geothermic spring

⛴   denotes a harbour with connecting ferry services

Road and path networks:

-     a continuous line denotes a metalled road
or unsurfaced track feasible for motors

-     a dotted line denotes footpath only

CONTENTS

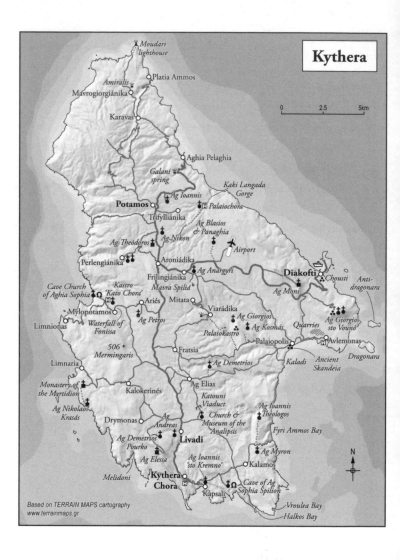

Kythera

0   2.5   5km

Moudari
lighthouse

Amiralis
Mavrogiorgiánika

○Platia Ammos

Karavas

Aghia Pelaghia

Galani
spring

Kaki Langada
Gorge

Ag Ioannis

Palaiochora

Potamos

Trifylliánika

Ag Blasios
& Panaghia

Ag Theódoros

Ag-Nikon

Perlengiánika

Aroniádika

Airport

Diakofti

Chousti

Anti-
dragonara

Frilingiánika

Ag Anargyrí

Cave Church
of Aghia Sophia

Kastro
'Kato Chora'

Mavra Spiliá

Ariés

Mitata

Ag Moni

Mylopotamos

Viarádika

Limnionas

Waterfall of
Fonissa

Ag Petros

Ag Giorgios

Ag Kosmás

Quarries

Ag Giorgios
sto Vounó

Palaiokastro

Palaiopolis

Avlemonas

506 +
Mermingaris

Fratsia

Ag Demetrios

Kaladi

Ancient
Skandeia

Dragonara

Limnaria

Monastery of
the Myrtidion

Kalokerinés

Ag Elias

Ag Nikolaos
Krasás

Drymonas

Ag
Andreas

Katouni
Viaduct

Church &
Museum of the
Analipsis

Ag Ioannis
Theologos

Fyri Ammos Bay

Ag Demetrios
Pourko

Livadi

Ag Myron

Ag Elessa

Melidoni

Ag Ioannis
'sto Kremno'

Kalamos

N

**Kythera
Chora**

Kapsáli

Cave of Ag
Sophia Spilion

Vroulea Bay

Halkos Bay

Based on TERRAIN MAPS cartography
www.terrainmaps.gr

KYTHERA

Famous in Antiquity as the island of Aphrodite, and immortalised as such in the European imagination of the 18th century by Watteau's celebrated painting *L'Embarquement pour l'Isle de Cythère*, Kythera still possesses something of the quiet enchantment which Watteau evoked. There is nothing particularly grand or showy here, yet no visitor can fail to be struck by the island's charm, or by the density and variety of its sights for its modest size: churches, landscapes, ruins, houses, caves, ravines, villages—there is no corner that is not rich in interest and beauty, natural or man-made. A longer visit than would at first seem sufficient for an island of this size, may well be necessary.

A glance at the map of Greece reveals why Kythera has had an enduring importance throughout history: it is the first refuge for ships heading into the eastern Mediterranean after rounding the often perilous waters off Cape Matapan, and is the obvious provisioning stop before the crossing to Crete and points further east. Today Kythera stands somewhat apart from the other Aegean islands: it belongs to no clear geographical group, although for a long time in its recent history it was administered together with the Ionian islands; nor is it on the ferry routes to any of the other islands, except for eastern Crete, whose colony it was in earliest Antiquity. It is close (20km) to the coast of Laconia, but its life and character are quite separate from that of the mainland; and today it is administered as a distant eparchy of Piraeus in Attica. All these links have in different ways enriched the island, but none has ever compromised its quite distinct cultural independence.

Kythera's most remarkable heritage lies in its numerous Byzantine remains and paintings, hardly surpassed in quality or variety anywhere in the Aegean outside Naxos. They have survived so well here because the Turkish occupation of Greece scarcely touched the island. They include not only unusual painting and architecture—such as the freshly preserved 12th century figures in the frescoed cave-church of Aghia Sophia below Mylopotamos, or the curious composite church of Aghios Demetrios at Pourko—but also whole settlements, such as the stunning site of the deserted Byzantine town at Palaiochora and the tiny Kato Chora of Mylopotamos. Other Byzantine remains—for example the enigmatic fragments of mosaic floor in the church of Aghios Giorgios at Vouno—go back as far as the 7th century, if not earlier. Often, too, what is mediaeval covers ancient antecedents: the primitive and quite extraordinary interior of the church of Aghios Kosmas at Palaiokastro, which stands on the probable site of the ancient Sanctuary of Aphrodite, is dramatically fashioned out of Archaic columns, capitals and fragments. And the church of Aghios Giorgios, mentioned above, rises over the site of a Minoan hilltop sanctuary almost 3,000 years its elder.

Kythera has numerous villages of great charm, with an attractive vernacular architecture. There are waterfalls, mills and verdurous streams at Mylopotamos and at 'Amir Ali' near Karavás; tranquil springs below Viarádika; and hidden grottoes and beautiful beaches, at many points around the coast. The island has good wine; the climate and vegetation foster a notably aromatic wild oregano and, above all, the island's exceptional honey which was famous even in Antiquity.

HISTORY AND LEGEND

As might be expected of an island as close to the Peloponnese as Kythera, archaeological evidence (from the southern cave of Aghia Sophia in particular) bears witness to settlement as early as the 6th millennium BC, becoming more widespread on the island in the 4th millennium. Lying on the route between Crete and the Peloponnesian mainland, Kythera was already subject to Minoan settlement early in the 2nd millennium BC. By the end of the 15th century BC the island had been abandoned by Minoan settlement, and a Mycenaean presence proliferates in its place. The name 'Kutira' appears in a list of Aegean place-names dating from the reign of Amenhotep III (c. 1400 BC): but Aristotle remarks that, in remote Antiquity, the island is said to have been called *Porphyrousa* ('the purple one') from the abundant *murex*-bearing molluscs in its waters (*see pp. 33–34*). The Phoenicians (c. 1100 BC) developed the island's purple industry and also may have introduced the worship of Syrian Aphrodite, as Herodotus (Bk. I, 105) suggests. This might explain Hesiod's account of the birth of Aphrodite as occurring just by Kythera in the *Theogeny* (l. 192). The island figures in the *Iliad* as the home of the two Achaean warriors, Amphidamas and Lycophron: the latter was killed by Hector, the former was one of those hidden within the wooden horse. The 5th century BC dithyrambic poet, Philoxenos, was also born on Kythera.

In c. 550 BC, Sparta seized Kythera from Argos, and during the Peloponnesian War the island guarded the southern seaboard of Lacedaimonia until it was subdued by Nicias for Athens in 424 BC. In 195 BC it was under Spartan dominion once again; but in 21 BC it was gifted to C. Iulius Eurycles by Augustus in gratitude for his support at the Battle of Actium, later being returned once more to Sparta by Hadrian.

Christianity may have come to the island in the person of the martyr, Aghia Elessa, in the 4th century. Archaeological evidence suggests well-established Christian communities in the 6th century, which were later given considerable impetus by the arrival of the Blessed Theodoros in the 10th century. After the Fourth Crusade, Kythera, mostly under the control of the Venetian family of the Venieri, suffered many invasions—the worst in 1537, when the capital was destroyed and the inhabitants sold into slavery by Khaireddin Barbarossa. The island remained a Venetian possession, however, referred to by its Italian name Cerigo, up until the dissolution of the Serene Republic in 1797, except for a brief interlude of three years of Turkish sovereignty, 1715–18. In church matters, however, the Orthodox Church maintained an almost absolute dominance.

After 1797, briefly captured by the French, then seized by the Russians, left in anarchy, and returned by treaty again to the French, it was eventually taken by the British in 1809, who administered Kythera together with the Ionian islands until their union with Greece in 1864. Kythera was the first piece of Greek territory to be liberated by Allied forces in September 1944. Since the Second World War the island has seen massive emigration to Athens, the USA and, most significantly, to Australia, where the largest overseas community of Kytherans today is to be found.

The guide to the island has been divided into four sections:
* *Kythera Chora and Kapsali*
* *Ancient Kythera and the southeast of the island*
* *Palaiochora and the north of the island*
* *Mylopotamos and the southwest of the island*

A note on visiting Byzantine churches on Kythera

The island, for its size, has an unequalled wealth of Byzantine churches. Many of those mentioned here are kept locked and their keys are no longer held, as before, by a local neighbour. This has become the case after a notorious series of thefts in the 1990s; and the policy is unlikely now to change. To visit, for example, four or five of the greatest treasures on the island outside the months of July and August, different entities or people will probably need to be contacted:

- the key for the cave church of Aghia Sophia, below Mylopotamos, is kept in the custody of the *Demarcheion* (the
  Town Hall: T. 27360 31213) in Chora, except in July and
  August, when the church should be open for four hours
  every day, except on Mondays;
- the keys for the ancient churches on the peak of Vouno
  are kept by the local *pappás* (priest) of the Palaiopolis parish (this parish includes the monastery of Aghia Moni (T.
  27360 33251) where he can often be contacted);
- for the painted churches of Aghios Demetrios at Pourko,
  Aghios Andreas at Livadi, or Aghii Anargyri and Aghios
  Vlasios at Frilingiánika, the keys are kept at the Byzantine
  Antiquities Department (T. 27360 31195) in the main
  street of Livadi, although the churches are occasionally
  open for liturgies or cleaning.

Those involved are generally helpful in facilitating visits: but
finding the right person at the right moment is not always easy.
The few churches mentioned above are of such importance or
beauty that the effort needed to get to see them will be more
than repaid; for the others mentioned in the text below, it is up
to the visitor to decide according to his or her stamina. Never
fail, however, to go into any church which happens casually to
be open for whatever reason, even if you are on your way some-
where else: the opportunity is golden.

KYTHERA CHORA & KAPSALI

The proper settlement of the Chora of Kythera dates
from the time of the abandonment of the early mediaeval
capital of the island—then called Aghios Demetrios and
now referred to as 'Palaiochora'—after it was sacked and
destroyed by Khaireddin Barbarossa in 1537. The town
seems small for the size of the island. Apart from the impressive castle and a couple of mansions and 17th century
churches, it consists mostly of small spaces and humble
dwellings. The setting and views are magnificent, however.
The town beetles along a high ridge which runs northwest
to southeast. From the small square of the town hall at the
north end, a single main street winds through the centre
towards the castle, passing an elegant late 19th century
communal **market building** on the way. A little beyond
this, is the church of the **Estavroménos** (the cathedral of
Kythera), with stone *campanile* and a simply carved doorway bearing the coat of arms of the Darmaros family: just
to its north lies the church of Aghia Anna. Both churches
are mid-17th century buildings and both have interesting
iconostases of the same date, as does the church of Aghii
Pantes, on the edge of the ridge further to the northwest.
The latter has fine views of the valley including the pic-

turesque ruins of the church beside the cemetery far below. After the cathedral church, the street passes under an arch, formerly the outer gate of the Venetian Kastro. An **18th century mansion** on the right beyond the gate has an elegantly carved door-frame and an elaborate and beautiful coat of arms carved in marble above the lintel, with *fleurs de lys*, crown and palms, flanked below by cannon to either side, dating from its use by the French Governorate at the turn of the 19th century.

The **Venetian Kastro**, impressive from the outside but a little soulless on the inside, presents a well-preserved enceinte of late 16th century fortification walls of the design and masonry typical of that period. The site, which dominates the natural harbour of Kapsali and the southern sea-passage round the island, had been fortified since at least the early 13th century, and we have notices of a castle here that was repaired by the Venetians in 1502. But it was only after the torching of Palaiochora in 1537, that the tiny remaining population who had survived Barbarossa's destruction moved here to settle in what must have seemed greater safety. The site was deemed of sufficient strategic importance to justify for the Venetians the expense which so large and powerful a fortress represents.

Today, the entry is by a broad 19th century ramp which

breaches the original walls: below and to the right of it as you enter is the former serpentine tunnel-entrance of the 16th century. The interior of the castle is open and ruined, and encloses a heterogeneous group of buildings in varying states of decay. On the left after entering is a pleasing ruined mansion of the Staïs family, currently being restored. All around a number of cannon are still in place: they bear the much eroded royal monogram of the British king, George III, and date from the capture of the island by the British from the French in 1809. There are also a few cannon from earlier periods; one, near the church of Aghios Ioannis Prodromos, is Venetian and bears the date 1684. This church and the unadorned **church of the Pantocrator** (further uphill on the right) both belong to the earlier, pre-16th century castle on this site. The ascent is crowned by a building—functional and military in its austerity—once used as the official residence of the British *chargé d'affaires* and known as the 'Palace of the Overseers': it now houses the extensive and valuable **historical archives** of Kythera. Passing through it, you come out in front of two churches, side by side: the larger is the church of the **Panaghia Myrtiodotissa**, formerly the Catholic church of Santa Barbara, built in matter-of-fact style by the Venetians in the 17th century. Abutting its north wall is the older orthodox church of

Panaghia Orphanon (or 'Madonna degli Orfani')—with a single (crooked) barrel-vaulted chamber. An extensive restoration campaign is currently under way at the Kastro. The site's greatest joy remains the beauty of its views down to Kapsali port and towards Antikythera, and, in spring, the abundance of flowering *campanula*.

The castle was the inner stronghold of a larger complex of civil habitation which clung to its northern and eastern sides. The walls of this outer area can still be seen in part on the slope which drops down towards Kapsali; and the densely populated area within them was known as **Mesa Bourgo**, 'the town within'. This is a fascinating and picturesque site; it is small and the lay-out is simple. It is reached by any one of the narrow alleys that descend from near the entrance to the castle, down to the steep eastern slope below the castle walls. Apart from stretches of the walls, only the churches now remain, and most of these are from the 14th and 15th centuries, indicating that this area was inhabited before the destruction of Palaiochora. The first church on the path is the church of **Aghios Athanasios**, which has fine 16th century moulding around the door on its south side. Further to the south and on the right, is the tiny single-aisled church of **Aghia Triada** (with small belfry): there are some relatively late wall-paintings in this church from 1610, with a well-preserved inscription, beside a diminutive figure below and to the right of the *Pantocrator* on the south wall, beseeching the Lord to 'Remember the soul of … Kasimatis Sanudo', the church's benefactor. Just beside and to the south is the church of the **Panaghia Mesochorítissa** (with double belfry). The ruined church of **Aghios Demetrios**, just beyond this, is the most accessible of the group: only its apse and the south wall of the nave still stand, but these both bear (eroded) early 15th century paintings of interest. With some clambering it is possible to get close enough to the paintings to see the remarkable fineness of execution of the faces. At the furthest point of the path (southern extremity) are three churches: **Aghios Giorgios of Kaloutzis** (with double bell-tower) and, slightly below, the two intercommunicating chapels of **Aghios Philippos** and **Aghios Ioannis Chrysostomos**. The first has paintings in the two blind arches on either side of its interior chamber: a rather ill-proportioned *Archangel Michael* of the 15th century, above the burial-place of Neophytos Kaloutzis (whose name has given the epithet to the church), and a beautiful *Dormition* scene painted perhaps a century later. The second (middle/south) church (Aghios Ioannis Chrysostomos) has an interesting ensemble of paintings on its north wall, with a small inset of a lady benefactress (in ?late 16th century costume), just below the finely modelled head of the horse of *St George*. Higher up the slope above these churches is the abandoned chapel of **Aghios Ioannis Drapanezis**. Returning towards the centre of Chora from Mesa Bourgo along Odos Kaloutzis, you pass a fine patrician Kytheran house, with garden and stone-mosaic patio in front.

Kythera's one-room **Archaeological Museum** (*open 8.30–3.30; closed Mon*) is on the edge of the Chora, just to the right of the road which heads north to Livadi. The museum is currently awaiting an overdue modernisation.

The artefacts here are few and not displayed to their best advantage, but they are not without interest. A strikingly beautiful vessel in steatite, as well as a small lamp, are evidence of the sophisticated Minoan presence on Kythera in the 2nd millennium BC, and of the fine materials they brought from elsewhere: there are also fragments of an unusual clay cooking-grill. Most of the exhibits, however, come from the coastal area of Palaiopolis (*see below*) and the site of Palaiokastro above it in the interior of the island. The room is dominated by an Archaic (6th century BC) lioness from Palaiokastro, with her tail curled neatly inside her right flank in a manner stylistically characteristic of Archaic design. There is no visible inscription—just later graffiti on the back of the head. The piece must be approximately contemporary with the lions/lionesses of Delos, but the rough cutting of the hind paws and the slightly awkward realisation of the shoulders mark it out as being of a less skilled workmanship. There are also many storage *amphorae* exhibited which come from different locations on- and off-shore around the island.

The beautiful double harbour of Kapsali lies 2km below Chora: it has shops, lodgings and several tavernas. At the eastern edge of the inner harbour, behind imposing iron gates, is the *Lazareto*, or quarantine station—a group of low early 19th century buildings around a cobbled courtyard, centred on a well-head and now picturesquely overgrown with figs, palms and bougainvillea— once used during epidemics and for mariners deemed to require reclusion. Looking back up from here towards the castle, the whitewashed face of the mountainside hermitage of **Aghios Ioannis sto Kremno**, is clearly visible in the cliff face to the north. (*This is reached by taking the road signposted 'Camping' to the right as you re-ascend towards Chora: just beyond the campsite entrance, a path leads up through the trees to the hermitage.*) The outer gate (with a marble plaque bearing a dedicatory inscription of the 16th century) leads to a low tunnel and to a steep flight of steps that climb up to a group of caves, the deepest of which has been rather roughly adapted into a church. This cave stretches some way into the hillside to the north. The rather dilapidated iconostasis runs flat along the east wall, facing you as you enter, and a tiny door at its south end leads directly up steps to a ledge which was the hermit's place of prayer. From all points there are striking views. The church is dedicated to St John the Theologian, and a tenuous legend relates that he began writing the Book of the Revelation here. This is the first of an unusually large number of cave-churches on the island (*see box pp. 74–75*).

ANCIENT *KYTHERA* & THE SOUTH EAST OF THE ISLAND

Most of the ancient sites on Kythera lie along or near to the southeastern coast, a fact which underlines the greater importance and interest of Crete, rather than of the Peloponnesian mainland, in the island's earliest history. In good weather conditions, Crete is visible from here and, with the stepping-stone of Antikythera at the half-way point, the sea journey between the islands was not difficult to undertake. The coast offers a couple of relatively sheltered anchorages, and there is a beauty and un-menacing quality in the wide sweep of its bays and the valleys behind, which must have appealed to early settlers.

At the eastern extremity of the island, a conical hill (356m) rises solitarily, offering splendid **views** towards the mainland, to Crete, and into the rising sun. Today the hill is crowned by the two whitewashed churches of the **Panaghia Myrtiótissa** and of *****Aghios Giorgios sto Vouno**; but on this commanding site in the 2nd millennium BC there was a Minoan mountain-top sanctuary. (*Access by 3km of unpaved road, leading southeast from the asphalt road at the summit above Diakofti. Keys for the churches with the* pappás *(priest) of Palaiopolis.*) The space at the top of the hill has a natural east-west orientation: its Minoan site was uncovered in 1992 right in front of the churches and stretching a few metres to the south onto the slope overlooking Avlémonas. The numerous finds indicated that the site was an important sanctuary, used continuously from the Minoan Bronze Age to Classical and Byzantine times. A considerable quantity of small Minoan votive idols with raised hands, made of bronze or clay, were discovered—notably more in bronze than in clay. These are now in the Archaeological Museum of Piraeus. This was the first such sanctuary to be found outside Crete, and the new light that it sheds on early Minoan trade and colonisation makes the work which was done here a very significant piece of archaeology. The dig has been covered over once again, and there is little of it to see now, but the church of Aghios Giorgios (the more easterly of the two), which contains some rare and curious *mosaics in its floor, provides great interest.

The mosaics are not extensive, but they are clearly visible—particularly when wet with water. They are executed in four colours of stone: one scene is of a huntsman in an oriental hat and elaborate red jacket, with a leopard and other animals and birds which are close to him but not clearly related in any narrative way; on the south side is a small roundel-shaped fragment with a booted and dressed figure, with a partridge and some different coloured flowers that have the appearance of bunches of grapes, beside him. The mosaic, behind the *templon* screen, picturing a dove enclosed within an abstract meander design, has a different style—much simpler and executed in only three colours, with a lower density of *tesserae* per area. The apsidal shape of its lay-out would suggest that it was contemporary with the construction of a church here, though not necessarily the one standing today; it may also be of a different (possibly later) date from the other mosaics. Both the costume and style of the hunting mosaics have suggested a generally accepted date of the 7th century AD; but an earlier date (even late 5th century) cannot be excluded. The mosaics raise many interesting problems: not least how to explain why such a remote site should have been so lavishly and unusually decorated in a period in which Kythera was a distant and poor outpost of civilisation. The subject matter is also perplexing: Christian interpretations can be given to its program, but the scene with the hunter seems particularly secular. This may simply show how slowly new imagery evolved, and how the old pagan visual motifs were still alive and well, although with a new significance, in the early Christian era. But it is not implausible that the mosaics belonged to a pre-Christian building on this site—possibly even a Late-Roman patrician villa—which is yet to be fully explored.

The existing 13th century church has a stone and plaster *templon* screen bearing the date 1882. The murals on the north and south walls are also 19th century, though breaches in the plaster reveal earlier layers beneath.

The adjacent church of the **Panaghia Myrtiótissa** (to the west) is in effect two churches: a square church of the Panaghia, surmounted by a shallow cupola of concentrically corbelled, rough-cut stone; and the later addition of the church of Aghios Nikolaos to its west side. Although the Panaghia is the oldest construction extant on the hilltop, and is of the 10th century or earlier, all the churches here are probably built over the foundations of earlier ones, which in turn cover the pagan structures beneath. As if to bring the whole ensemble into modernity, the double church of Aghios Nikolaos/Panaghia Myrtiótissa has, in its otherwise bare interior, a pleasingly *naïf*-style iconostasis, dated 4 December (St Nicholas's day) 1908.

The two islands just off-shore, visible from the peak of Vouno, are **Dragonara** (south) and **Antidragonara** (north). Archaeological finds on the latter are providing evidence that it was the home of an important sanctuary to Poseidon '*Gaieochos*' (γαιήοχος, 'earth-upholding'). A quantity of votive vases and coins with provenance from all corners of the Mediterranean and Black Sea regions show that this minuscule islet was a focus of considerable cultic significance in later Hellenistic times. Due north of the peak of Vouno, another tiny island, Makrikythera, has been joined to the main island by a bridge to form the new port of **Diakofti**. (The beached hulk of a Polish vessel, which ran aground in 1999 on the rocks of Prassonissi just outside the port, after an evening of revelry in the mess, provides an encouraging welcome to the harbour.) Near Diakofti is the cave known as *'**Chousti**', a fascinating natural pothole with an underground sanctuary, which is currently in the process of being excavated and studied. (*200m inland of the bridge at Diakofti, a small* *road leads off to the east; after 150m it ends and becomes a track. Following the track up onto a slight rise, the unobtrusive entrance down into the cave is at a point about 50m north of two stone, barrel-vaulted churches.*) Steps, carved in the rock, lead down into the cave which has a spacious round form, like a cupola, illuminated by a roughly circular breach at its apex. The form suggests the dome of the heavens with a solar oculus in its centre. The floor of the cave has vestiges of simple masonry, now collapsed and partly buried. Excavations are beginning to uncover layers which show that the cave has been a place first of refuge and later of cult, from Neolithic times through to the Geometric and Classical eras. One of the most curious finds to come from the cave is part of a clay tablet incised with lists of syllables, used probably for the teaching or practising of writing by a student. The foundations of an ancient building are visible outside the cave, just to the west of its entrance but standing more or less over the chamber below. The building, or temple, was rectangular, approximately 12 x 8m, and oriented perfectly to the cardinal points.

The peak above Diakofti is crowned by the imposing monastery of **Aghia Móni**, built in 1840: the ornate bell-tower, which dominates the spacious courtyard, is in carved *poros* stone. (*8.5km inland from the bridge at Dia-*

kofti, turn uphill 3km to monastery.) The *catholicon* has a fine façade, which contrasts with the plain front the monastery presents to the road as you arrive. In 1806, Theodore Kolokotronis took refuge in the dilapidated monastery on this same site when he came to Kythera fleeing from the Turkish authorities; he prayed for safety and promised to rebuild the monastery should he live to see Greece liberated. The bust and monument to him at the junction of the road leading to the monastery, celebrates his fulfilment of that promise.

Returning to a point on the main airport–Daikofti road, 4.3km inland from the bridge at Diakofti, a concrete road leads downhill towards the coast and to Palaiopolis. The valley you descend into is a limestone honeycomb of caves, holes and shallow gorges. There are also many **ancient limestone quarries**: these are mostly superficial, but are clearly visible today from the road, imparting a strangely 'cubist' form to the landscape in places. One large area of quarrying is visible to the landward side of the coast-road just before it enters Avlémonas. **Avlémonas** has grown up around a tiny natural cove which was once a principal port of the island. It was just out to sea from here that Lord Elgin's ship, *Mentor*, carrying a consignment of the Parthenon sculptures *en route* for London, sank and had to be raised from the sea-bed in

1803. There is a fine octagonal 16th century **Venetian fortress** on the promontory which guards the entrance to the port. The picturesque harbour is dominated by the 18th century Cavallini mansion, with an elaborate sundial over its entrance: this building served as the Austro-Hungarian consulate in the early 19th century. The fact that the clear waters of these bays are sometimes referred to as *Loutra Aphroditis*, or 'Baths of Aphrodite', is witness to the persistent tradition that the goddess's remarkable birth happened nearby.

APHRODITE

Aphrodite, the goddess of love and the protectress of sexual union and reproduction, is often given the epithet '*Kythereia*', and the island, in turn, is sometimes referred to as 'the Island of Aphrodite'; the two—goddess and island—are closely associated. In contradistinction to Homer's account of the goddess as daughter of Zeus and Dione, Hesiod's *Theogeny* (ll. 188–206) describes how she was born from the foam that splashed up where the severed genitals of her father, Uranus, fell to the sea—namely, off Kythera. From this (appropriately) messy beginning, Hesiod goes on to describe how she was wafted by waves to

Cyprus where she came ashore and was venerated as the protecting divinity of the island. This improbable story may be seen as the Ancient Greeks' way of appropriating and Hellenising a divinity whose origins lay undoubtedly in the East and whose cult may have been brought by Phoenician traders and settlers via Cyprus to Kythera. Herodotus says (Bk. I, 105) that he had reason to believe that the temple of Aphrodite at *Ascalon* (modern Asqelon in Israel) was the most ancient of all her temples anywhere, and that '…the one in Cyprus, the Cypriots themselves admit was derived from it, and the one in Kythera was built by the Phoenicians, who hail from this part of Syria'.

The cult of Aphrodite is as complex as love itself and many different aspects of the goddess were venerated in different places: she was known as '*Pandemos*' in Athens, protecting the continuity and fertility of the whole community; as '*Euploia*' in the Aegean ports, protecting mariners on the sea from which she herself was born; as the dark '*Melainis*', the patroness of carnal love and prostitution, and the powers of the night, in Corinth; and, here in Kythera, as 'Aphrodite *Ourania*' or 'heavenly', presiding over every kind of union—especially those of a higher nature. Sanctuaries to Aphrodite in particular attracted the destructive attentions of early-Christian zealots, and it is not surprising therefore that very little remains of her temple here on Kythera. But her presence in, and association with, the island has been given momentum in the Western imagination by the fame of Watteau's whimsical painting, *L'Embarquement pour l'Isle de Cythère*, painted in 1712/3—a work which was crucial in bringing his extraordinary talent to the attention of a wider public. It created an indelible picture of an imaginary Kythera for generations of Europeans who, like Watteau, had never been to the island.

Herodotus's words, quoted above, could suggest that Avlémonas might be, in origin, a Phoenician settlement— perhaps the site of the ancient port which bore the name of 'Finikounda'. But evidence of a Phoenician presence has always been characteristically elusive, and may simply derive from the fact that Kythera was famous in classical antiquity for the production of purple dye from the murex shell—an industry and trade that was particularly associated with the Phoenicians.

MUREX PURPLE DYEING

The technology of dyeing textiles in a rich purple colour derived from marine molluscs is remarkably ancient. It has always been supposed that it was first mastered by the Phoenicians or the Minoans around 1600 BC; but there is archaeological evidence which suggests that is was possibly developed a century or so earlier in the Persian Gulf, and perhaps subsequently brought into the Mediterranean by the Phoenicians. The origin of the dye is in a colourless fluid in the hyperbranchial gland of the *Murex brandaris* and *Murex trunculus* molluscs: this fluid is actually the precursor of the dye, and when exposed to the atmosphere it converts rapidly to the purple pigment. The technical difficulty lies in the fact that, once it becomes a pigment it is no longer soluble, and in order properly to dye a fabric the colouring matter must be in solution. The chemical technology involved in circumventing this problem, which involved fermentation at high temperature, has always been a well-kept secret: even Pliny the Elder, in the 1st century AD, was unable fully to obtain the necessary information for his encyclopaedic *Natural*

History. With the fall of Constantinople in 1453, the purple-dyeing industry was so effectively destroyed that the art of the dyers was lost, and it was only by chance rediscovered again in the late 17th century. The waters around Kythera and in the gulf of Laconia are rich in the *murex* mollusc which is required in notably large quantities for the process. It was for this reason that the Phoenician or Minoan settlers of the 2nd millennium BC in the bay of Palaiopolis may have established their dyeing commerce in the area. To this day it is still possible to find murex shells amongst the potsherds along the shore.

The coast road leads back, west from Avlémonas, to **Palaiopolis**. This name refers to an extensive coastal area which includes, amongst other things, the site of the ancient city of *Skandeia*, whose exact location has not been determined. The long, wide sweep of its bay is interrupted to the southwest by a headland called 'Kastrí', where numerous excavations have taken place. The extreme southwest corner of this headland has small caves which show signs of adaptation for the purpose of cult and of burial in ancient times. But it is in the area to the south of this point, and as far as the next promontory of

'Kastraki', that the presence of *Skandeia* is most evident. Beyond the river-bed that flows into the beach, the density of potsherds in the back wall of the bay is evidence of substantial settlement here in Antiquity: pieces of vase, tiles, and *murex* shells can still be found on a cursory inspection. Ancient *amphorae* and *pithoi* were once so plentiful here that many of the traditional baking ovens of the houses in this area were lined with them. In the rocks at the south end of the bay, below the headland of Kastraki, are a number of man-made, deep holes used for lodging and fixing wooden capstans to which boats could be tied: there are several more on the top of the promontory. The material evidence points to this area having been continually inhabited from the beginning of the 2nd millennium BC right through to Byzantine times.

Just west of Palaiopolis the asphalt road divides and, 200m down the left-hand fork, an unmade road leads off to the left through olive groves towards the sea. Shortly after passing the church of Aghios Minás, the track ends (1.5km), and steps lead down to the beautiful and protected beach of **Kaladí**.

The bay of Palaiopolis (or Aghios Nikolaos), has the mildest climate in the island because it is protected by a ring of hills behind. Today, this interior is a wild and uninhabited area; its dense *maquis* covers vestiges of ancient tombs, as well as hidden Byzantine hermitages. It is on the most prominent of these hills behind, known as **Palaiokastro**, that the probable site of the ancient sanctuary of Aphrodite, mentioned by Herodotus, is to be sought. Pausanias, who remarks (III.23.1) that the sanctuary was the oldest place of the cult of Aphrodite in the Greek world and that the goddess here was figured fully armed, estimates that it was at a distance of 10 stades (approximately 1.8km) from *Skandeia*. The exact site has never been definitively located, even though it has attracted the attentions of great archaeologists—foremost amongst them, Heinrich Schliemann, who came here to dig in 1887 together with Valerios Staïs. Schliemann concentrated his trial excavations in and around the isolated church of ****Aghios Kosmás** (also referred to as Aghii Anargyri). This is the most fascinating and tangible monument here because it is clearly constructed out of architectural elements taken from an ancient temple, possibly even the temple of Aphrodite itself. The church is difficult to reach—at certain times of year a machete is necessary; but it is of such interest that the effort is fully repaid. (*At the junction in the road just west of Palaiopolis on the coast, take the right-hand fork for Fratsia. The road climbs and, after 3.3km, levels out before beginning to descend a little, just as the view of the interior of the island opens before you;*

at this point, to the right (north), an unsigned track leads up the hill of Palaiokastro. From this point of departure, however, Aghios Kosmás itself is not clearly visible; by taking the asphalt road 500m further towards Fratsia and looking back, you now see the profile of the hill clearly, with the tiny church of Aghios Giorgios crowning the summit, and Aghios Kosmás—the object of this visit—on the shoulder of the hill below and to the east. Access is not always easy and lies partly through dense undergrowth: a stick and good boots are advisable. The walk can take 50 minutes each way from the main road.)

The track ends after 400m in a flat area just below a small deserted stone house. On the ground here is an ancient carved stone basin and well. Beneath the dense undergrowth all around are the collapsed walls and numerous terraces of an area which was densely inhabited in Antiquity, probably the acropolis of the ancient city. Some recent archaeologists (Coldstream & Huxley, 1973) have suggested that the temple of Aphrodite was located 'on a terrace mid-way between Aghios Kosmás and the chapel of Aghios Giorgios at the summit of the mountain'. This is just above where you are now standing.

Aghios Kosmás is clearly visible from here, and is best approached by continuing on the level towards the east and striking uphill to the church at the very last moment.

This is a tiny abandoned isolated and cramped church with no external embellishment or grace whatsoever; but few churches in all of Greece give more poignant expression to the period of turmoil after the collapse of the Graeco-Roman world, when pagan temples were unheedingly pulled down and their elements used in new buildings to the new Deity. The crude exterior of Aghios Kosmás consists mostly of uniform rectangular blocks taken from ancient buildings, with some few truncated columns also incorporated, and supplemented with rough stone filling. Inside, it is dark and has the feel of a prehistoric cave. The *interior structure of the church dates in all probability from the 6th century AD—although it has been reinforced, retouched and redecorated many times since then. The narthex appears also to have been added at a later date. It is divided (almost as an ancient temple might be) into three successive zones, and the tiny interior space is dominated by the four supporting Doric columns and the disproportionate blocks of ancient masonry on all sides. Schliemann found that two of these columns had not been moved from their original position, and concluded that the church had therefore been built directly over a pagan temple. A couple of the capitals are well preserved, and these, together with the fact that the columns are monolithic, would suggest an early (Archaic) date for the temple to which they belonged. The lintel block over the

passage between the narthex-area and the central part of the
church is a re-used and inverted piece of ancient architrave:
on its inside (east) face, the decorative dentils are still visible. Both long walls and the area above and between the two
apses have the very eroded remains of paintings, but with
their colours still quite fresh in places. A design with two (as
opposed to one or three) apses side by side at the east end
is not particularly usual, and in this church it may reflect
the dedication to the two Anargyri, or 'money-less' saints—
SS. Cosmas and Damian, who travelled in Syria and in Asia
Minor offering their medical services gratis. This particular
dedication may also be reflected in the presence of a long
low stone 'bench' along the inside walls of the church: part
of the early cult of these two saints involved the practice—
adopted from pagan forebears—of 'incubation', in which the
sick would sleep in the church hoping for a dream in which
the saints would visit them to cure them of their infirmity.

Generally in the early-Christian world, where there was
previously a temple dedicated to the Dioscouri—the divine
twins and 'saviours' of Antiquity, Castor and Polydeuces
(Pollux)—we find a church honouring their Christian coun-
terparts as twins and saviours, Cosmas and Damian. Until
the site is explored in greater detail, it is not possible to say
whether this remarkable church marks the spot of a temple
to the Dioscouri or is built on the site of the temple of Aph-

rodite—or whether the antique elements in it come from one, or both, or neither of these possible temples.

At the summit of the hill of Palaiokastro is the church of **Aghios Giorgios**. (*There is no clear path and a visit is only for those with stamina and determination.*) This is a much later, single-aisled church of the 15th century, and is therefore not comparable with Aghios Kosmás below. The whitewash of the interior of the church has flaked away to reveal only small traces of wall-painting in the conch of the apse, depicting the Virgin. On the plateau to the west of the church, however, the foundations of a sanctuary to a female deity have been identified, and finds on the site indicate that it was frequented continuously from the 8th century BC through until Hellenistic times. The **views** which the site commands are magnificent and worthy of any great, Ancient Greek acropolis.

Regaining the asphalt road and continuing towards Fratsia, you pass the church of **Aghios Nikolaos**—unadorned, but constructed in fine stone-work—which stands to the left (south) of the road after 1km. A further 2km beyond, on the hillside and summit to the right (north), the quantity of walling and ruined stonework would suggest fairly dense habitation here in mediaeval or earlier times. The road finally reaches a plateau and then comes to Fratsia after a further 2.2km. At this point, two itineraries are possible: the first, a loop to the north; the second to the south and returning to Chora.

1. North loop

A right turn in Fratsia leads north towards the village of **Viarádika**. Immediately on entering this village, a road to the left is signposted to 'Vrissi Aghiánnis': this leads through the village and ends at a point where there are plentiful springs of a soft water. Close to the spring is the tiny **chapel of the Metamorphosis**: the whitewash in the interior has flaked away to reveal fragments of 13th century painting of considerable quality, with some beautifully realised faces and details just visible. A path continues beyond into a **limestone gorge**, whose walls are perforated with natural caves and man-made hermitages: the area has a striking geographical similarity to the gorge and Bronze Age site of Pantalica in Sicily.

After Viarádika the road descends steeply and then, as it climbs up again towards Mitata, the cliff-side of the gorge comes into view, with the cave hermitages and the remains of their retaining walls still standing, visible in the rock-face. **Mitata** is a quiet, rambling village with several fine houses in the island's simple and dignified vernacular architecture. This is also a good place to find

Kythera's famed **honey**. From the *plateia* by the church of
the Taxiarch Michaïl, are wide views over the plateau and
hills to Aghios Giorgios sto Vouno, and beyond.

In the area of **Frilingiánika**, to the north of Mitata,
are two pairs of contiguous twin churches, both with
fine paintings and both dating from the 12th and 13th
centuries: together they make an interesting comparison because of the different styles of the painters working in them. First, the church of the **Aghii Anargyri**,
on the main road. (*A little over 2km north of Mitata, the
road comes to a junction with the main airport road, close
to the village of Frilingiánika. Turning right at this point,
the church is immediately on your right, at the exit from
the village.*) There are two parallel churches here—contiguous and intercommunicating, joined by a transverse
vaulted narthex—both of which contain extensive fragments of 13th century wall paintings. The interest here
is mostly in the appreciable individuality of one of the
painters, whose style is best seen in the *Ascension* scene
which covers the barrel vault before the apse in the south
church: his is not an especially sophisticated style but he
has imparted to the simplified and elongated lineaments
of the faces of the saints a memorable clarity and character peculiarly his own. Their exophthalmic gazes are,
at the same time, both distant and intense. This style is

quite distinct from those found in the next pair of twin churches. (*Two kilometres further on towards the airport, a signed track to 'Aghios Vlasios' to the left (north), leads 1.5km across the top of the treeless plateau to the churches.*) Again these are two contiguous and communicating churches—**Aghios Vlasios** (north; 12th century) and the church of the **Panaghia** (south; late 13th century)— which lie in a largely deserted area known as Pente Pigadia, just west of the airport. It would seem that the north church of Aghios Vlasios and its paintings are the earlier, from the fact that the wall-painting of *St Irene* on the south wall was destroyed when the arch was opened to communicate with the south church. Both churches are barrel-vaulted and single-aisled, both have an identical configuration of double apses, and both are decorated extensively with wall paintings. Here the faces have a wholly different character: *St Blaise* himself, and *St Niketas* in the two apses, or the full-length figures of *St Mamas* (with lamb) and *St Theodore* (mounted), above and to the right as you enter, have a greater uniformity and roundness of face than those of the 'Anargyri painter', but they are nonetheless quite individual in style. The paintings in the south church, executed around a century later, are again very different—heavier, more formal, richer in pigment and altogether more metropolitan in feel. The artist who

painted the richly ornamented throne of the Panaghia, or
Virgin, in the apse, or the figures of SS. Stephen, Myron
and Basil just to the left of it, does not share the freshness
of the earlier painters. His style has a more official kind
of solemnity to it.

Returning to Frilingiánika and taking the left (east) turn
towards Mitata once again, the right-hand fork, shortly after this leads to Aghios Ioannis and the Spiliá Mavrá or
'Black Caves' (*signposted*). Aghios Ioannis is a superficial
grotto that has been turned into a church with marble
screen. Its roof is the natural rock of the cave. Down the
dust track, towards the west, are the '**Black Caves**'. (*The
track shortly turns left (south), running parallel with the
ravine. The caves come into view, high up on the left-hand
side. After 150m, the meagre remains of a stone-walled construction are visible in the undergrowth to left: from here a
path leads steeply up to the caves.*) There are principally
two caves. The southern cave incorporates the remains of
a Byzantine oratory, with an apsidal cut in the rock and
meagre vestiges of wall paintings, bearing a not-fully legible inscription referring to the '...Great Martyr, George...'
The northern cave has the remains of mediaeval walling
both in its entrance and inside, where the rock has been
cut at the north end: the interior once had a spring or pool
in it. How ancient these caves are as places of dwelling and

refuge is difficult to establish with certainty; but their saintly occupants in the Byzantine era were probably only the latest in a long tradition of worshippers here.

(*Regaining the asphalt road from here and turning to the right (south) brings you to Mitata and to Fratsia once again, at which point the road continues on the second itinerary, eventually returning to Chora.*)

2. South loop

South from Fratsia for Aghios Elias. (*In village of Aghios Elias, left turn at narrow cross-roads for Palaiopolis and Kalamos, then subsequent left fork (to east) for Palaiopolis. After 1.5km Aghios Demetrios is signposted down track to left.*) The early 13th century church of *Aghios Demetrios lies in open country, isolated and with fine views down the gorge towards Palaiopolis. The presence of substantial ruined buildings nearby, suggest that this church was once the *catholicon* of an imposing monastery. The church today is a simple cube with an attached apse, surmounted by a cupola—the dome occupying almost the whole of the area of the *naos*. The interior is dominated by the huge and impressive, early 13th century depiction of a youthful and finely robed *St Demetrius* with both hands raised in prayer, flanked by *Two Donors*—a man (in black clothes) and a woman (in extravagant finery), both apparently wearing plain white hats on their heads: these hats were probably decorated originally with *appliqué* decorative elements which have since been removed. The fine murals of the dome and on the walls belong to subsequent campaigns of painting, of the late 13th and 14th centuries.

Retracing the route back to the junction and continuing south to Kalamos, the road continues through a number of villages, all bearing names with the characteristic, Kytheran '-iánika' ending—Goudiánika, Travasariánika, Skouliánika etc. (In most cases, these names are formed by adding the suffix '-iánika' to the name of the founding family of the village; most of these families were encouraged by the Venetians to stay and re-settle the ravaged island after the depredations of Barbarossa in 1537.) Shortly after, the road crosses a narrow gorge at Katouni on a stately arched **stone viaduct**, looking uncannily like something you might expect to find in the Tweed Valley. Simultaneously functional and beautiful, the 13-arch span of the bridge was built in 1828/9 by the Scottish engineer John MacPhail, as part of a network of communications lines and improvements planned under the British administration to give the Ionian islands the infrastructure necessary for economic growth. The extant lighthouses and school-buildings on Kythera were also part of this overall plan.

A short distance beyond the bridge, the road comes to a wide junction with the church of the Analipsis (Ascension) on the left, in the settlement of Kato Livadi. The small building on the north side of the church houses the island's **collection of Byzantine and post-Byzantine art**. (*Open 8.30–2.30; closed Mon.*) This is a small collection of icons, ecclesiastical objects, and detached wall-paintings (from many of the churches mentioned in this text), beautifully displayed and clearly illuminated. The collection rotates, so it is not possible to predict exactly what will be on show. But customarily exhibited are: the apsidal painting of *St Andrew* from Aghios Andreas, Livadi (13th century); a group of standing *Saints* from Aghios Ioannis in Potamos (13th century); *St Nicholas* from Aghios Petros, Arei (13th century); *St Catherine* from Aghios Antonios in Palaiochora (16th century). Here also is the important fragment of early Christian floor mosaic from Aghios Ioannis in Potamos, and a number of beautiful 17th century icons, amongst which is a fine *St John the Baptist*, showing Cretan influence.

THE DETACHMENT OF WALL-PAINTINGS

Detaching a fresco or wall-painting is a traumatic business for an ancient work of art: it involves adhering a linen cloth with a slow drying soluble glue to its painted surface. This holds the pictorial layer complete and integral while the plaster on which it is painted is physically sliced away from an older layer of plaster or from the wall behind it. Once free of its support, the painted surface, now held and bound temporarily by the cloth, is transferred to a new wall or panel (in this case, one suitable for museum display). A solvent is then applied to the cloth to release the glue's adhesion to the paint surface, which is now again held integrally by its new support. The process is best avoided if at all possible, but it may be necessary in two kinds of situation: if the painting is in danger because of imminent structural collapse of its supporting wall or from exposure to weather or chronic infiltration of water (as is the case with the paintings taken from Palaiochora); or if it is felt necessary to reveal a lower, older layer of painting beneath by removal of the covering layer (as in the case of some of the paintings here from Aghios Andreas, Livadi).

Four kilometres south from the junction at the church of the Analipsis, the road comes to **Kalamos**, after passing an impressive stand of cypress trees in the valley below. Here, as in Mitata, there is good local honey for sale. From Kalamos a sign-posted road leads east down to the coast at **Fyri Ammos**, a long and beautiful, but exposed, stretch of beach. By the (second) road junction, 2.8km from Kalamos and 2km inland from the beach, a path leads south to the minute and hidden 14th century church of **Aghios Myron**. The church is built on a steep gradient and the whole south side consists of one huge sloping buttress, as if to stop the building sliding down the hillside. The tiny dark interior measures about 4 x 2.5m, traversed by a partially painted *templon* screen in masonry. The best-preserved paintings, dating from not long after the church's construction, are the figures of saints on the lateral walls. The track which heads due north from the junction at this point leads to the isolated and panoramic church of **Aghios Ioannis Theologos**. This is an interesting example of a church whose cupola, surrounded by a tall 'collar' of masonry, also serves as a watch-tower. This is the best-preserved example of a phenomenon called a *'vardiola'* which was relatively common on the island and served to keep a look-out against the constant danger of pirates.

From Kalamos, the main road leads back west to Kap-

sali and Chora, along a high ridge with views to the south.
1.2km west of Kalamos, a road off to the south descends
steeply through cypress and olive groves into a ravine,
and brings you (1.8km) to the impressive **cave of Aghia
Sophia of Spiliés**. The cave, with a modern chapel in its
entrance, is wide and has some venerable stalactites and
stalagmites in its depths. It is not surprising that this nu-
minous spot has yielded evidence of the earliest human
settlement on the island in the form of pottery datable to
around 5500 BC. There is almost unbroken continuity of
human presence here up into the late Bronze Age.

Just over three kilometres (by track) beyond Aghia
Sophia to the south is the pretty and protected beach of
Halkos; further still to the east, and accessible by 4km of
track from Kalamos, is the beach and cove of Vrouléa.
Returning to the main asphalt road above Aghia Sophia,
however, and turning west will bring you to Kapsali and
to Chora after 4.5km.

PALAIOCHORA & THE NORTH
OF THE ISLAND

(The main north/south road of the island is joined by the road from the airport and the port of Diakofti at a junction in the centre of the island at Aroniádika. This is the point of departure for this itinerary of the north of the island.)

Less than 1km north of the junction at Aroniádika, a road (subsequently unmade) leads northeast across a plateau to *Palaiochora (4km). The setting of this deserted Byzantine settlement is courageous, magnificent and unexpected. Much of the interior of Kythera is on an undulating plateau; at this point, however, a number of streams have carved precipitous ravines which have their confluence here, plummeting 250m to the sea below, through the gorge of *Kaki Langada* (or 'evil defile'). The fortress and settlement of Palaiochora clings to a central dividing spur of the gorge. The few remaining and abandoned churches are built precariously over vertiginous drops; the vigorous vegetation is colourful in all seasons, the aroma of wild oregano overwhelming, and, if the wind is still, the only sound is of echoing bird-song and the omnipresent buzz of bees. The view extends across the sea to Cape Malea and the Peloponnesian mainland. In the foregound as you approach, and all around, are the remains of (what was then called) the town of Aghios Demetrios, the hidden and seemingly impregnable capital of the island from the 13th century through until its complete destruction by the Turkish admiral Khaireddin Barbarossa in 1537.

(Of the three churches here which still have their roof and walls complete, and which are often kept locked, one alone (Aghios Antonios) has some remaining decoration in the interior. Only someone with specialist interest need take the trouble to obtain the key from the Archaeological Office in Livadi, should the buildings all be locked: the beauty of the setting and the ruins outweighs the interest of these interiors.) Just below the path and to its north is the beautiful free-cruciform profile of the church of **Aghia Barbara**, with its high octagonal drum and cupola still intact and roofed with irregular slabs of schist, and its three symmetrical facetted apses. The bare interior has an unexpected spaciousness in spite of its small size, perhaps because it is free of any piers supporting the dome, which here sits firmly on the corners of the crossing. Both viewed from outside and in its inside, this is a perfect example of the best 13th century Byzantine, church architecture.

The path descends to a saddle which gives access to the

fortified 'acropolis' of the city. To the left is the church of the Panaghia tou Forou (still in use), with a masonry *templon* screen and a somewhat dissonant modern roof. Further in, and just below the walls of the main fortification, is the late 15th century church of **Aghios Antonios**, with a belfry and elegant ogival door-frame on the north side, which leads into a very irregularly shaped ante-chapel, before giving onto the main naos. The apse of the church (as can be seen from the outside) is on the verge of collapsing; some of the paintings (a 16th century *St Catherine*) have been removed to safety and are now on exhibition in the church/museum of the Analipsis in Kato Livadi (*see above*). Those that remain are in a condition as precarious as the church itself. The masonry templon screen is decorated with fluted pilasters, and bears vestiges of painting, with a very faint kneeling *Donor figure* at the lower north corner.

The keep-gate, just above Aghios Antonios, is not easy to discern: most of the settlement's defence, in any case, lay in the natural site more than in massive walls. On all sides around the fortified spur, over a dozen churches have been identified, several of them hanging from the cliff-edge. Almost at the peak of the hill is a larger, roofless church of the 14th century which still bears some fast-vanishing paintings *in situ*, and is believed to be dedicated to the city's patron, **Aghios Demetrios**. Just to the east, the land drops below the walls in a sheer fall into the gorge. Further round, to the north side, a long barrel-vaulted chapel (possibly dedicated to the Taxiarchis Michaïl) has slightly better preserved 15th century paintings in its vault. The best wall-paintings from each of these two churches have now been detached and are on show in the museum of the Analipsis. Few houses are visible at Palaiochora, but the extant remains of some larger civil buildings may be seen just to the east of the Panaghia tou Forou.

Returning to the main north/south road and heading 500m further north beyond the turn for Palaiochora, a small road-side oratory marks a left turn (west) to the **monastery of Aghios Theodoros** (300m), containing the relics of the 10th century spiritual father, Theodore of Kythera, who left the mainland, settled on Kythera and died here. The spotless façade of the *catholicon* is dominated by an intricate and heavily **carved escutcheon** in high relief—a particularly fine, southern Italian work of the early 17th century. There are angels with scrolls holding a crown above the elaborately framed coat of arms. The minute inscription below the feet of the right-hand angel refers to a certain lord (bishop) Athanasios, whose arms these may be. Sadly, a late 19th century restoration of the interior of the *catholicon* has left the original 13th century foundation all but invisible, except in its form and in the presence of a damaged fresco at the north end of the *templon* screen. In the northwest corner of the church is the reliquary of St Theodore. The elegant and imposing building to the north of the façade of the church was built by the British in the early 19th century as a school. It is one of several on the island, all of which are different and are not without architectural merit.

A further 500m to the north beyond the junction by the oratory on the main road, the solitary profile of the 12th century church of **Aghios Nikon** is visible in a field to the right (east), containing patchy remains of wall-paintings, mainly in the squinches of its low and irregular cupola, and in its two unsymmetrical apses of different sizes. Even the base of the (now dismantled) *templon* screen is not perpendicular to the (unparallel) walls. The tiny church is a hymn to the Byzantine love of irregularity.

Almost opposite Aghios Nikon, a road leads off the main road to the west, towards the village of **Perlengianika** (1.5km). Here, on a slope at a little distance to the south of the road, are two churches, not contiguous but linked by the remains of a square tower which once stood between them. The north church of **Aghios Andreas** is of the late 14th century; the tower and the south church of **Aghios Giorgios** are nearly a century later. The area

covered by wall-paintings in both churches is considerable, but their condition is poor. This is due to mineral
efflorescences which make the pictures hard to read. Most
visible of all is a striking scene in Aghios Andreas of the
Entry into Jerusalem, in the vault of the *naos*. The extraordinary and amusing hats and robes of the little children
strewing and collecting palms do not detract from the
magnificent presence of the Christ figure against a deep,
night-blue background.

Many of the villages in this area—**Aloiziánika**, **Za-
glianikiánika**, **Pitsinades**, and especially **Trifylliánika**—
have interesting vernacular architecture of the 17th and
18th centuries, and are a pleasure to explore on foot.
Their principal point of reference is **Potamós** (2km north
of Aghios Nikon), the capital of the north of the island.
Sufficiently far inland to have avoided the less penetrating
depredations of pirates and marauders, and sufficiently
far north to have a distant similarity to the southern Peloponnesian villages across the water, Potamós is also quite
different in appearance from Chora: there is less the feel
of the 'island bastion' here. The presence of a number of
13th and 14th century churches in the vicinity, shows that
Potamós was substantially inhabited at the same time
as Palaiochora, to which its citizens would have moved
when it was necessary to seek protection and refuge in

times of danger. But the recent (1990) discovery of Early Christian floor-mosaic fragments in the dilapidated 13th century church of Aghios Ioannis, near the village's cemetery, has suggested that the settlement here is far older, going as far back as the 6th century perhaps. (*The mosaic is now in the church/museum of the Analipsis in Kato Livadi.*) Today Potamós is a thriving and pleasant village, more lively than beautiful, with a number of large neoclassical houses which possess grand airs, but rather lack a proper context.

To the north of Potamós, the road passes into more fertile land at the northern extremity of the island, descending after 8km into a well-watered valley at **Karavás**. The beauty of the springs here can best be appreciated at **Amir Ali** (a strange Turkification of the Venetian word 'Ammiraglio', referring perhaps to an admiral who resided in the vicinity): a well-signposted, narrow road leads down here from Karavás. There are plentiful springs, plane trees, a café and an ensemble of pleasing 18th and 19th century houses—some inhabited, some in ruins. At **Mavrogiorgiánika**, on the hillside above, are more examples of the local architecture of the same period—simple, square, well-proportioned houses with low-pitched roofs, similar to those in the southern Peloponnese. A 4km walk with fine views, north from Mavrogiorgiánika, brings you to the early 19th century **lighthouse** at Moudari, built by the British: this marks the northern extremity of the island.

The northern branch of the asphalt road ends 3.5km beyond Karavás at Platiá Ammos, a small seaside resort with beach: the south eastern branch leads back to **Aghia Pelaghia** (5km), which was formerly the main port of the island up until the opening of the new harbour at Diakofti. Following the coast line to the south, and continuing once it becomes a track for a further 2km, you come to the seaward **outlet of the Kaki Langada** gorge which descends from Palaiochora, at Limni where the track terminates below cliffs rising 200m above. A bar of pebbles blocks the freshwater descending from the gorge and forms a small pool at the narrow exit. There are small colonies of samphire on the cliffs, with only marginally less flavour than the famous Chiot samphire. The gorge, viewed from here, is impressive; but it can only be entered if you are prepared to wade some distance.

The main road south from Aghia Pelaghia climbs rapidly, passing another small cave-church dedicated to Aghia Sophia, and, slightly higher up, the Spring of Galani. It then levels out on a plateau, thick with pine woods. Five and a half kilometres from Aghia Pelaghia and less than 1km from Potamós, to the right (north) of the road and isolated in a field, is the 13th century, double-church of

Aghia Kyriakí, which in the apse of its south chapel has four large painted faces of saints—among them Aghia Kyriakí herself. At the same point on the main road, a sign indicates a track leading 200m right (south) to the church of Aghios Ioannis in the pine woods. This is another double church of later date (15th century), with fragments of painting inside. The frequent occurrence of double or twin churches on the island is the result of demographic changes. The earliest rural churches are largely tiny structures; and in periods of relative stability (e.g. before the devastations of Barbarossa in 1537 and again in the mid-17th century) when the population notably increased, rather than pull down an often beautifully decorated church and build something bigger, a parallel church would be added to one side in order to accommodate the larger congregation.

Just as you enter Potamós once again, the road passes over another of the **stone bridges** built by John MacPhail in the 1830s under the British administration, similar in design to the much larger viaduct at Katouni (*see p. 46*), but this time more beautiful—its central arch wider than the others and unexpectedly decorated with fine carved swags of fruit and foliage. Four kilometres south of Potamós, the road returns to the central junction at Aroniádika, where the itinerary began.

MYLOPOTAMOS &
THE SOUTHWEST OF THE ISLAND

Heading out on the main road north from Chora, the sea soon disappears from sight and the road enters the fertile and protected **valley of Manitochóri** which lies just behind the town. This must always have been Chora's 'back garden', providing much of the produce which the town lived off. It is still productive to this day, though it is now dotted with more churches and houses. To the west, the hill of Lionis rises steeply; here, Valerios Staïs—the 19th century archaeologist who had been given the difficult task of officially supervising Heinrich Schliemann's activities while he was digging at Palaiokastro (*see p. 36*)—uncovered a Minoan tomb and its artefacts from the 16th century BC, giving substance for the first time to historical knowledge of prehistoric Kythera.

At 3.5km from Chora is **Livadi** the functional and commercial centre for the south of the island. (*A right turn from the middle of the main street, leads directly (1km) to the Byzantine Church/Museum of the Analipsis— see above. Just beyond this turn on the right hand (east) side of the main street is the office of the Byzantine Antiquities Department which holds the keys for many of the Byz-*

antine churches under their protection on the island.) In both Kato (lower) and Ano (upper) Livadi, and on the road which joins them, are a number of fine mansions of the 18th and 19th centuries. Of entirely non-indigenous style, by contrast, is a curious rectangular building (now abandoned) with large gothic windows and half-crenellations, which is visible on the top of a hill to the west, less than 1km north of the town on the main road towards Potamós. This is one of the several **school-buildings** on the island, constructed as part of the plan to improve the island's civic infrastructure during the British Administration, between 1809 and 1864. The architect was clearly in Tennysonian mood at the time.

In close proximity to Livadi are two of the island's most interesting Byzantine churches. A signposted road to the west from the middle of the main street of the village leads to the church of **Aghios Andreas**, which sits on a rise about 150m from the main road. The church has a pleasing profile, broad and low, with a belfry that has been added in the last 100 years. It dates from the second half of the 10th century, originally square in plan with three apses, but shortly afterwards extended slightly towards the west. The paintings inside are fragmentary and concentrated around the sanctuary, but they are of high quality and belong to different campaigns of work by clearly different hands. A number of the paintings from later (17th century) layers have been detached and transferred to the Byzantine Museum of the Analipsis in Kato Livadi. Where this has happened, the pitted layer of the earlier wall-painting beneath is visible *in situ*; the regular chips and holes made with a sharp instrument in the surface of the older plaster facilitated the integration or 'keying-in' of the new plaster which was to be super-imposed. This can be seen in the central apse and on the front of the *templon* screen. Two different artists, indeed two different ages, can be seen in the area of the sanctuary beyond the screen. The pale colours, exiguous brush-strokes and more simple but vital facial descriptions of the paintings above the central apse, and in the fragments of the north-side of the northern apse (*prothesis*) are of a painting campaign contemporary with the construction of the church (10th century). By contrast, the figures on the opposite south wall of the northern apse (*Aghios Minas*, for example) and the altogether graver faces, darker colours and higher contrast of the figures in and around the north and south side walls of the sanctuary and in the barrel vault overhead, belong to a campaign of the 13th century. The contrast of simplicity and freshness, with gravity and ornamentation, is immediately visible.

An altogether more complicated picture is presented

by the extraordinary church of ****Aghios Demetrios** at **Pourko**—Kythera's most interesting Byzantine monument. This is one of the most unusual churches in the Aegean, in some ways comparable with the (much earlier) church of the Drosianí on Naxos. (*In Livadi take the left fork, signed for Aghia Elessa and Moni Myrtidíon, at the point where the main road turns towards the right and to the north. Keeping left at the junction after 1km, you come to the locality of Pourko after a further 1.8km. The church of Aghios Demetrios is in the valley below and to the left, 250m down an un-surfaced track.*) The setting of the church can best be seen by carrying on up the road to the monastery of Aghia Elessa, a large modern monastery on the peak with very fine views, which remains uninhabited for most of the year. From here the church of Aghios Demetrios is visible in the fold of the fertile valley below: its site suggests something that is often the case with dedications to St Demetrius—that the church may originally have been built over a pagan sanctuary of Demeter, whose places of cult often lay well outside habitation and in fertile valleys where the cereals which the goddess protected were cultivated. From closer to, the church seems like an enormous piece of sculpture; its organic growth and undulating volumes possess a plasticity of great appeal. All this is due to the fact that the church is not one, but four churches in

one building—all of different sizes, different forms, with
different orientations, and yet contiguous, intercommunicating and possessing only one entrance between them
all. The reason for this bizarre arrangement and seemingly
unplanned propagation of buildings is unclear, but it raises
interesting questions about the 'logic' of church building
in the Middle Ages in Greece. The most probable explanation for the organic 'agglutination' of chapels in the case
of the Drosianí on Naxos, mentioned above, is that the
main, pre-existing church there was the funerary chapel of
some important holy individual, around which the others
all clustered. But this seems a less likely explanation here:

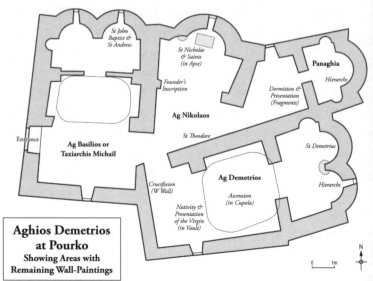

St John Baptist & St Andrew

St Nicholas & Saints (in Apse)

Panaghia

Hierarchs

Founder's Inscription

Dormition & Presentation (Fragments)

Ag Nikolaos

Entrance

Ag Basilios or Taxiarchis Michaïl

St Theodore

St Demetrius

Crucifixion (W Wall)

Ag Demetrios

Hierarchs

Ascension (in Cupola)

Nativity & Presentation of the Virgin (in Vaults)

Aghios Demetrios at Pourko
Showing Areas with Remaining Wall-Paintings

0   1m

N

the earliest church of the four that comprise Aghios Demetrios (the south church) shows no funerary characteristics.
There is nothing comparable to the highly unusual arrangement here, and little clue to explain its development.

Chronology

The entrance is in the west wall of the last of the four churches to be built. You first enter (1) the *northwest church*—oriented due north; dedicated either to St Basil or the Archangel Michael; dated to the late 13th century; with small
dome and two apses, (later) segmental *templon* screen in
masonry, and paintings of figures of saints, principally to the
right in the sanctuary. From here you pass into (2) the *north
church*—oriented a little to east of due north; dedicated to
St Nicholas; dated to the mid-13th century; with one apse,
and extensive fine painting remains in the apse and sanctuary in particular. Passing directly on from here, you enter (3)
the tiny (2 x 3.7m) *northeast church*—oriented a little north
of due east; dedicated possibly to the Virgin; dated to the
mid-13th century; with one apse and only fragmentary and
poorly preserved paintings. Returning to the north church,
you pass (left) into (4) the *south church*—oriented almost
due east; dedicated to St Demetrius; dated to the early 13th
century; with dome and two apses, and extensive and fine
wall-paintings in most areas.

The paintings

A start at unravelling the dates and campaigns involved in the painting can be made in the north church of St Nicholas, where, on the pilaster in the middle of its left-hand (west, in this case) wall, is a partially legible dedicatory inscription which cites the names of a founder (Nikolaos Kontodonatos) and—unusually—a painter (Archdeacon Demetrios of Monemvasia). Scholars have tried to read a lost date at the foot of the inscription which has led to an erroneous dating of the paintings (and therefore of the whole complex) to the late 12th century: in fact the inscription is referring to an ecclesiastical indiction of 100 years later. All this need not distract the visitor from the enjoyment of the vibrant paintings of finely-robed saints on the same wall of the church, and of the arresting design of the figure of *St Nicholas* in the apse, all of which is the work of Demetrios of Monemvasia. In the south church there are probably three layers of paintings, which in places (e.g. the north apse) can be seen one below the other: but these layers are separated by a matter of decades only. Unusually, there are a number of larger narrative scenes in the church: a *Crucifixion* on the west wall, a *Presentation of the Virgin*, an *Annunciation* (below the dome), a *Nativity*, etc. The richer pigments in these scenes and in the figures in the apses, combined with the artists' delight in costume and architectural detail, suggest that Kythera had begun to have closer artistic ties with the imperial capital, Byzantium, than it had ever had before in its history.

Two kilometres north of Pourko is the village of Drymónas. From here it is possible to visit two monasteries, both with 19th century buildings and fine views of the western coast of the island. Immediately to the west, over the hill, is the monastery of the Aghii Anargyri (1.7km), built with forbidding defences against coastal piracy. Beyond it, a track winds down (3.5km) to the minuscule cove and secluded beach at **Melidoni**. The road north of Drymónas leads to a junction (after 1.2km) beside a dense stand of pine trees, in which a fine **neoclassical mansion** operates as an *oinopoieíon*, or winery. Turning left (west) here, you pass through the whitewashed village of **Kalokerinés**, descend a succession of plateaux, pass through an improbably precarious rock arch over the road, and continue down (5.5km) to the **monastery of the Myrtidíon**, amongst dense green *maquis* on a slope above the wild western coast of the island. It is unclear at what date a monastery was first established here to celebrate the finding of a miraculous icon in a myrtle bush (hence the name 'Myrtidíon'); the present buildings and the interesting carved limestone bell-tower all date from the late 19th century. The monastery is still busy and well cared for, and its courtyard bursts with plants, trees and flowers. The *catholicon* is remarkable mostly for its marble elements: a capsule-shaped pulpit, an orientalising stand for the sacred icon, and eight polished plaques in the lower part of the templon screen, all of an unusual, alabastrine grey stone.

Nearly two kilometres further north, the asphalt road ends at the beach of Limnária. A separate track to the south from the monastery leads (2km) to the remote chapel of **Aghios Nikolaos Krasás**, built by a grateful shipper of wine (*krasí*) after successfully supplicating St Nicholas to save him when he and his entire shipment of wine seemed in danger of foundering on the cliffs below during a storm.

Either by returning all the way to the winery and turning north, or by taking the left fork in Kalokerinés, you join a small road that heads north, for just over 5km, through a cultivated valley to *Mylopotamos—to many, the most beautiful village on the island. Once home to over 1,000 inhabitants, and now a village of about 100 souls, Mylopotamos (which means 'mill river') is characterised by its abundance of water—running through the village, feeding the vast plane trees in its square, falling in a beautiful 20m waterfall, and once servicing nearly two dozen mills along the length of the gorge below. This water seeps in springs from the *poros* limestone mountain of Mermingáris (506m) to the south of the village. The mountain, and consequently the water source, is currently threatened by a proposal for industrial quarrying on its slopes. The village has a pleasing combination of handsome neoclassical mansions and more traditional stone houses, haphazardly grouped around the ravine: at its centre is a peaceful shaded *plateia* with a delightful *kafeneion*.

For the **mills** and the **waterfall of Fonissa** it is necessary to take the street which leaves due north from the *plateia*; after 150m a wooden sign to the '*Katarráktis*' points down some steps to the right. This leads down into an enchanting densely-shaded gorge with a number of ruined buildings, emerald pools and gigantic trees. The impressive—because unexpected—waterfall is to the right. Further downstream are the water mills, of which there are over 20 (in varying states of disrepair) in the valley, all once working from the same re-used water. One of them (about 400m downstream) is currently being restored: it has a narrow stone-built fall-chamber with a horizontal turbine at the base, which turns one millstone against another fixed stone above it. Outside the building the stone rings may be seen to which the mules and donkeys would be tied.

Eight hundred metres to the west of the village is Mylopotamos's mediaeval centre and *kastro* at **Kato Chora**. The
first building you come to, as the road makes an abrupt
about-turn to the left, is a decently proportioned spacious
hall with gothic ogival windows—seemingly mediaeval
but in fact another British school-building, constructed
by John MacPhail in 1826. Directly behind it, however, is
the finely rusticated **entrance gate** into the Venetian *kastro*, with the emblem of St Mark in marble and coats of
arms bearing the date 1545 above. This is a castle where
the emphasis is far more on habitation than on defence.
On entering, you find yourself in a narrow street, amidst
intimate spaces and mediaeval buildings which have been
enlarged and adapted in later centuries; they still preserve
their work areas (e.g. masonry tanks for wine-ferment-
ing, baking ovens and animal stalls) below, and the living quarters above. Most have pleasing window and door
frames; some have balconies. Almost half of the habit-
able area of the *kastro* is occupied by churches, however,
which squeeze into the space available, as if manoeuvring
to elbow one another over the precipice. These are generally kept locked, but only two of them have substantial
decoration inside and are worthy of the trouble involved
in having them opened (*keys with the Byzantine Antiquities Department in Livadi*). Going clockwise around the

inside perimeter of the enceinte, you pass: the church of Aghios Athanasios; Aghios Ioannis Pródromos, leaning like a sinking ship, and with paintings inside; Aghios Vasilios; the church of the Transfiguration (Metamorphosis Soteras), with its acutely rhomboid plan; (from here the chapel of Aghia Marina is visible opposite, across the valley); Aghios Ioannis Chrysostomos on the edge of the precipice, and Aghii Kosmás and Damianos, set down below it, against the walls. In the centre are two further churches of the Panaghia Mesosporítissa, and of Prophitis Elias. All date from the period between 1450 and 1550. **Aghios Ioannis Pródromos** can probably be dated more accurately to 1518 on the basis of a partially legible inscription in the fragments of paintings on the south wall. The church's elongated form is due to a considerable enlargement to the west. Particularly noteworthy is the mural of the two mounted, soldier saints (*SS Theodore* and *Stratelates*) at the western end of the south wall, with sensitively modelled faces and considerable chromatic intensity. The church of the Transfiguration, or **Metamorphosis Soteras**, is somewhat earlier—late 15th century. Its south wall and vault have extensive wall-painting remains in poor condition: an exception is the very fine figure of *St John the Theologian*, towards the western end of the south wall.

As you continue further down the asphalt road below
Kato Chora and the Venetian Kastro, east of the small
bridge is the minute 14th century church of the Archis-
trategos (St Michael), in the midst of an olive grove. After
1km, a track to the right leads down a further 1km to
the *cave church of Aghia Sophia. (*Key is kept at the De-
marcheion/Town Hall: T. 27360 31213 in Chora, except in
July and Aug, when the church is open Tues, Thur, Sat & Sun
11–3; Wed & Fri 4–8; closed Mon.*) This is an exceptional
site and the most interesting of the many cave-churches
on the island. The magnificent position of the cave, in a
wide cliff-bound bay directly above the sea, suggests that
it could well once have been an early hermitage. The cave,
which is entered from a flight of steps, is about 100m
deep with stalactites and stalagmites in the interior. But
nothing quite prepares the visitor for what is to be found
immediately inside—an irregular *templon* screen (about
1.9m high), constructed in rough masonry and rendered
in plaster, which runs from side to side of the cave, and
whose beauty is in the exquisite **paintings** which cover it.
These have been remarkably well preserved by the constant humidity and temperature within the cave; they
possess a freshness of colour and finish which is rare to
find in painting of this antiquity. To the left is a small *St
Panteleimon* (bust only); then *St Sophia* (Holy Wisdom)

herself, and her three daughters *Agape* (Charity), *Elpis* (Hope) and *Pistis* (Faith); to the right is a *Deësis* (Mary, Jesus and John the Baptist), flanked by *St Theodore of Kythera* to the left and *St Theodosius* to the extreme right. On the perpendicular sides of the door through to the cave are: *St Nicholas* to the left, and the *Archangel Michael* to the right. A little further in the cave and down to the left is the sanctuary, in which there is a poorly preserved fragment of a painting of the *Virgin Mary*. The patterns and tones and colours of the native rock at times make the whole cave seem as though it were painted.

The setting itself is unusual, but the quality of these 12th century paintings is even more unusual, and it is worth looking at them closely. The painter has a clear style and very confident hand, but he also possesses a humanity which reveals itself exclusively in the figure of the local saint, **Theodore of Kythera*. This is a fine face, imbued with wisdom and suffering, and realised in paint with the most economical means. It makes the other faces, which are technically good, seem lifeless by comparison. Fortunately, a tiny inscription, between the figures of Christ and his mother, tells us about the painter, and informs us that his name—significantly—was also Theodore. In the inscription he asks for help from God—for himself, his wife and child.

CAVE CHURCHES

On Kythera alone there are no fewer than three cave churches dedicated to Aghia Sophia or Holy Wisdom (at Mylopotamos, Spilies and Aghia Pelaghia); two others on the island are dedicated to St John the Divine, Aghios Ioannis Theologos; and there are many more, both here and on other islands. Caves were always significant places of cult in pagan antiquity and earlier, and mystic rites were often conducted in them; they were seen as places of cosmic energy and of metempsychosis—symbolic passages for souls leaving the earth. They were sacred to many divinities. Christianity, as was its wont, appropriated pagan cult in caves to its own ends, but transformed its meaning. It was able to draw upon a rich philosophical tradition going back to Plato, in which the cave symbolised the ignorance and darkness of the lower world in which our souls are trapped. Our lives can be given sense, Plato suggested, by an ascent out of that darkness and by a purification of the mind and soul by adherence to divine wisdom. Divine wisdom—or Aghia Sophia—was therefore the only salvation which pierced the gloom of the primaeval cave where our souls were mired, and the path out was led by observance of Faith, Hope and Charity— Sophia's 'daughters', who appear here in the paintings in the cave at Mylopotamos. St John the Divine, author of the *Revelation*, is also associated with and venerated in caves because he received his revelation of divine wisdom in a cave on Patmos. In icons, St John is always pictured in the centre, as the conduit of illumination between the invisible Almighty above the top of the icon and his faithful scribe, Prochoros, hunched, writing in a cave in the lower part of the icon. Caves, in Christian iconography, are symbols of the state of our unillumined souls, and we go into them to seek wisdom and illumination for when we leave.

Beyond the cave, the road winds on down to the tiny port of Limniónas. Returning to Mylopotamos, and taking the eastern route (left) out of the village, after 1km you come to Aréi, where at a junction beside an Italianate chapel a track leads right (south) down a pine avenue to the isolated church of **Aghios Petros**. This is possibly an 11th or 12th century church, in un-dressed stone, with a pleasing profile and roughly square plan. It has three apses; its octagonal cupola was probably added later. In the paintings inside we encounter a new artistic personality—a painter who has particular difficulty with arms and hands. There are several layers and periods of painting in different areas of the church, but the work in the sanctuary is mostly of the mid-13th century and the work of one artist. His memorable style is characterised by a number of distortions of proportion in the neck and limbs. Below the central apse figure of St Peter is a founder's inscription. The church is of pleasing architectural form both inside and out.

A kilometre and a half further east you rejoin the island's main highway, at which point Chora lies 11km due south.

PRACTICAL INFORMATION

801 00 **Kýthera**: area 277sq.km; perimeter 118km; resident population 3,532; max. altitude 506m. **Port Authority**: T. 27360 34222 (Diakofti), 33280 (Aghia Pelagia). **Travel and information**: Porfyra Travel, T. 27360 31888,www.kythera.gr

ACCESS

Olympic Air runs one daily flight between the island and Athens throughout the year. Otherwise access is by sea from the southern Peloponnesian ports of Neapolis (one mid-morning ferry daily, making the journey in 1hr: T. 27340 22660 & 24004); Gytheion (four sailings per week—3 hrs: T. 27330 22207); and, more occasionally, in summer from Kalamata (5 hrs). These last two routes continue on to Kisamos (T. 28210 28217 & 24147) in eastern Crete, from which there is the same frequency of return connections. There are also weekly connections with Piraeus by ferry all through the year, and by hydrofoil in the summer months. Most boats now dock at the new port of Diakofti on the east coast of the island, 31km from the island's capital, Kythera Chora.

LODGING

Rooms for rent can be found in many of the villages on the island: the hotels, however, are mainly concentrated in or near Kythera Chora and at the port of Kapsali below. Particularly peaceful and with a good and panoramic terrace for breakfast, is the **Hotel Margarita** just off the main street in Chora, in the 19th century house in which Valerios Staïs, the archaeologist, was born. Open all through the year. (*T. 27360 31711, fax 31325, www.kythira-margarita.com*). Nearby, at the entrance to the Kastro of Chora is the small **Pension Nostos**, with half a dozen select, simple, well-appointed rooms of great charm (*T. 27360 31056, fax 31834, www. nostos-kythera.gr*).

EATING

In Chora it is not easy to find both good food and a pleasant setting together. **Zorbas**, in the main street, is known locally for its baked lamb at weekends, and the family-run **O Salonikos**, on the main road, has commendably fresh dishes at reasonable prices; but both places slightly lack atmosphere. One of the best tavernas to eat at on the island is **Skandeia** at Palaiopolis: it has excellent fresh wine, freshly-caught fish, and a variety of home-made, vegetable *pittakia*; the owners are welcoming and the setting is shady and beautiful. At nearby Avlemonas, *Korali* also has good fish. Kapsali has a number of adequate tavernas, of which **O Magos** is perhaps the best.

For Kytheran **honey, Yiannis Protopsaltis** at Mitata is recommended.

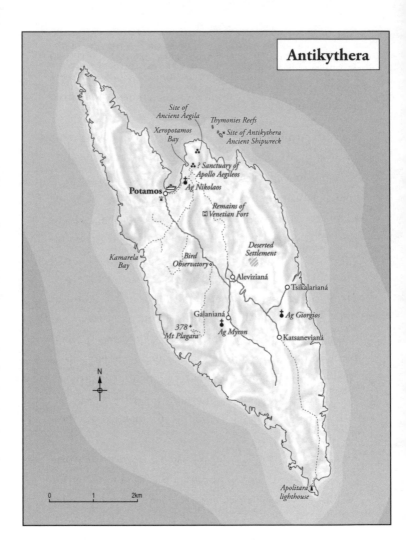

Antikythera

Site of
Ancient Aegila

Thymonies Reefs

Xeropotamos
Bay

Site of Antikythera
Ancient Shipwreck

? Sanctuary of
Apollo Aegileos

Potamos

Ag Nikolaos

Remains of
Venetian Fort

Deserted
Settlement

Kamarela
Bay

Bird
Observatory

Alevizianá

Tsikalarianá

Galanianá

Ag Giorgios

378
Mt Plagara

Ag Myron

Katsanevianá

N

0   1   2km

Apolitara
lighthouse

ANTIKYTHERA

Were it not for the fame of the unexpectedly rich finds that were made at the underwater site of a shipwreck which occurred in the 1st century BC off the northeast coast of Antikythera and gave the world the life-size bronze figure known as the *Antikythera Ephebe*, as well as a remarkable clock-like machine thought to be the earliest surviving astronomical computer in history, this island would be even more unknown and unvisited than it presently is. With around 40 permanent inhabitants, (currently) no hotel, no taxi, no bus, no taverna, nor even a dedicated *kafeneion*, the island is not an obvious holiday destination. But it makes an unforgettable—and not difficult—visit for anyone interested in peace and quiet, undisturbed archaeological remains, or ornithology. Antikythera, like so many of the very small islands of the Aegean, is a stepping stone. The settlers here who founded Ancient *Aegila* on the island took advantage of that fact, living off the trade and passage between Crete and the Peloponnesian mainland. Countless generations of birds, too, have seen a similar advantage in the island's strategic position as a resting place on their migrations between the continental mainlands of Africa and Europe. A visit to the extensive

site of Ancient *Aegila* and a walk through the interior of
the island to see its villages and bird-life, are—beyond the
sheer joy of its tranquillity—the principal reasons for vis-
iting Antikythera. The island also has excellent wine and
spring water, as well as good honey.

Antikythera is a little over 8km in length and just under
3km in width; in the centre of its west coast, Mount Plagara rises to a peak of 378m. Fresh water is not plentiful,
and the fertility of the land is limited. The island is linked
by name, and by a shared administration, to Kythera; but,
whereas Kythera has always tended to look north to the
Peloponnese for its commerce and cultural contacts, Antikythera looks firmly in the other direction to Crete. Its
inhabitants, who call the island 'Liï' (Lioi—a corruption
of 'Aigilioi') are of Cretan origin, with Cretan manners
and Cretan names. The mountains of Crete are indeed a
beautiful sight across the water from Antikythera.

HISTORY

Antikythera was a vital stepping stone on the route from
Bronze Age Crete to Kythera and the mainland beyond, but
little evidence of Minoan settlement has come to light so
far. The island appears seldom in ancient sources, though
Plutarch in his *Parallel Lives* (Cleomenes, 31.1) states that

Cleomenes III, king of Sparta, after his defeat by Antigonus III of Macedonia at the Battle of Sellasia in 222 BC stopped on *Aegila* on his way into exile in Egypt. At that time the island's Hellenistic city must have had a population of perhaps as many as 750–1,000 inhabitants. The island was probably under the authority of Phalarsana on the west coast of Crete. For much of its history, however, Antikythera appears to have been a base for pirates: Rhodian warships were engaged against them at the end of the 3rd century BC and may have razed the city in that campaign. Later, Roman forces under Pompey in the 1st century BC finally succeeded in eradicating piracy. It was at, or just before, the time of these Roman campaigns that the ship with a cargo of stone and bronze sculptures, amphorae and other objects, foundered and sunk off the northeast coast of the island. Known as the 'Antikythera Shipwreck', its discovery in 1900 and its celebrated finds mark the beginnings of the fruitful science of submarine archaeology.

Antikythera has a deep, relatively protected natural harbour in the north of the island, but the space in it for manoeuvre is limited, and most of the ferries (except the *F/B Andreas* from Neapolis) will turn round fully in the sea outside the entrance and enter the long, narrow channel of the port astern—an interesting operation to witness in a high sea.

The island's principal village, **Potamos**, is clustered in the valley and on the hillside behind the port; its name (meaning 'river') derives from its seasonal torrent and the presence of the only constant source of flowing water on the island. Just to the right of the landing stage is the former **water-mill**: the cistern above and water-chute are still intact, with the mill-machinery building at the foot of the drop, at sea-level. The **spring** which provides the water rises at a fountain in a small amphitheatre of rocks about 300m inland (to south), and sustains a number of productive gardens in the area: the year-round water is unexpectedly soft and light, and has good flavour. The small church to the west of here is Aghios Charalambos: plain and whitewashed inside, like all the chapels on the island, it has a simple but pleasing iconostasis. Further uphill is the church of the Panaghia.

The island's main settlement in Antiquity, *Ancient Aegila*, lies on a peninsula to the north and east of Potamos, its ruins just visible (to the eastern side) from the boat as it enters the port. A footpath leads up from Potamos along the side of the headland to the white church of Aghios Nikolaos, one of the oldest on the island. As you go down the slope to the east of the church, the presence of scattered potsherds all around suggest that this hill-side was also part of the area of ancient habitation.

Below is the ravine of Xeropotamos (named 'dry river' for obvious reasons), which ends at the pebble beach which forms a small harbour within the main bay. The shore-line in Antiquity would have been further inland since the level of the water was then substantially higher (*see below*). On the hillside opposite, you see a clear, diagonal path leading up to the ancient town. At the base of the hill which you have just descended (west side of the beach)— there is evidence of dried springs which may once have provided water for the ancient town.

Just inland, on the floor of the valley and in the final sweep of the riverbed, can be seen the partially uncovered foundations of a sanctuary, probably of the **temple of Apollo *Aegileos***: the presence of a well-cut square marble platform, a finely dressed stone well-mouth, and sundry blocks of marble suggests there was a public building or temple here, although the orientation of the building is not on the cardinal points. In this area a headless statue of Apollo (now in the National Archaeological Museum in Athens) with a dedicatory inscription to the god from two citizens, one Athenian and the other Thessalian, was discovered in 1880.

Climbing up the diagonal path above the east side of

the bay, there are several carved niches in the rock face to the right; a quantity of potsherds can be found all around. At the top there are steps, cut into the rock, which lead into an area which was once a protected gate of entry. A plateau now opens out in front: the walls around the acropolis are visible crowning the hill to the right, the remains of the lower town are in front, and the bay, below to the left. In the main area in front and to the right, there are many points at which the natural bed-rock has been substantially cut and dressed; this, together with the use of natural fissures in the limestone, was for the storage of water and of goods. The most interesting and legible part of these ruins is straight ahead at the edge of the sea, where a clear, broad ramp descends steeply to the water's edge: this is an ancient **boat-loading bay**. In examining this, it is important to remember that the whole island appears to have been pushed up by tectonic movement above what would have been the water-level in Antiquity. The entire coastline of Antikythera has a dark band just above sea-level which is approximately 2.5–3m in height, with furrows formed by successive sea-levels. It is hard to know exactly how much of this rise has taken place since the 4th century BC, but in order to make sense of this loading bay, allowance has to be made for a substantial rise in the land or drop in sea-level since that time.

There are clear signs (chisel striations) of the cutting of the stone on the floor of the ramp, the walls to either side, and the area immediately above and to the left (west). At the bottom of the ramp is a deeper cut to the right-hand side, which would have allowed one (shallow draft) boat to enter and be secured while loading and unloading onto the mole at the left-hand side. Just above this point is a deep transverse cut in the rock, running from side to side of the gullcy, and possibly used for securing winching equipment attached to the boat. The berth and the whole surrounding area is remarkably well-preserved.

Directly uphill from here, to the east, is a hole affording entry into a small underground chamber, neatly cut with two *loculi* or tiny chambers, to south and east. A round well-hole in the centre, underneath an opening above with dressed stone—possibly in the floor of a structure that stood above—suggests an underground *nymphaeum*. In fact, the whole of this area shows signs of terracing in the bare rock for the creation of cisterns.

The **acropolis** of *Aegilia* was on the ridge and the saddle to the north. Today this apron-shaped plateau is entirely surrounded with the visible remains of an enceinte of **Hellenistic fortifications**. The walls vary between 1.50 and 3m in thickness, and the ring of bastions or watchtowers is well-preserved—five are clearly visible, all are square, except the northernmost one which watched over the entrance to the harbour and was circular with a diameter of approximately 4m. In the middle of the area which the walls surround is a long narrow fissure in the rock: this was most likely a cistern for collecting water, given that it lies at the lowest point within the enceinte.

Towards the summit to the south extends a stretch of wall, typical of the style of construction of the 4th century BC: above this, the remains of three rings of walls are visible, which protected the highest point: the bastion on the peak (fortified mostly on the north side) is in rougher stone. The peak itself is interesting, and suggestive of a place of earlier cult: steps cut in the living rock lead up to a small flat surface which marks the highest point (90m a.s.l.) and which is oriented exactly on an east/west axis. Below it more steps lead up from an empty cleft in the natural rock. From here there is a good view of the *Thymonies* **Reefs**—the rocks just off the coast below and to the east where the shipwrecked ancient boat with its precious cargo was found in 1900.

THE ANTIKYTHERA SHIPWRECK

The large boat with a cargo of luxury goods, including jewellery, furniture and pottery, as well as a quantity of marble and bronze sculpture, which was possibly headed for delivery in Rome, ran aground and sank off the *Thymonies* rocks on the north coast of Antikythera some time between 80 and 50 BC. The wreck was discovered at a depth of almost 60m by a sponge diver, Elias Stadiatos, in 1900. It was one of the first significant underwater finds of lost cargos which have since become such a new and rich source of untouched material in the archaeology of the last 100 years. The finds are all now in the National Archaeological Museum in Athens. Most famous is the complete bronze statue of a fully life-size nude youth, in remarkably good state of conservation and with his glass-paste eyes still in place—the so-called *Ephebe of Antikythera*. The slacker musculature of the body and the bland, slightly oval face, indicate that it is a piece of the mid 4th century BC. The figure has his right hand raised aloft; in it he obviously once held something—a silver apple, if we wish to reconstruct him as the shepherd-prince

Paris of Troy; or perhaps the head of Medusa, if we wish to see him as Perseus, the Gorgon-slayer—in which case his lowered left-hand would (uncharacteristically) have held his sword. A fine, furrowed and unkempt head of a 'philosopher' in bronze, of the late 3rd century BC, was also amongst the finds. Most unusual of all, however, were the remnants of a curious and complex mechanical object, in which almost 30 bronze gear-wheels can be detected. This incomplete but elaborate computing device appears to have possessed a mechanism based on the epicyclic movements described by Hipparchus of Nicaea and Apollonius of Perge, which enabled it to show and predict the movements and positions of the celestial bodies, locating them on a circular dial with the constellations of the zodiac around its perimeter. It could well have been used for navigational purposes on the ship. If the machine did truly function well, then it managed to achieve all this with the added impediment of positing a geocentric cosmos as point of departure for the calculations. It is exhibited in the National Museum of Archaeology in Athens.

The acropolis walls subsequently descend from the summit to the south towards an area of recent (now deserted)
habitation; some of these houses have been constructed
using elements taken from the walls and are often raised
directly on ancient foundations. At the southern extremity of the enceinte a deep cleft in the limestone, below the
eastern side of a small outcrop of rock, functioned in Antiquity as a large communal cistern. The remains in this
area are harder to read because ancient pieces have been
moved and re-arranged by recent inhabitants seeking to
make threshing circles and animal pens, but several cisterns with spouts into rock-cut basins still preserve their
ancient appearance. At the southwestern corner of the
site the walls re-emerge clearly, and a gate is visible with
a path running down to the ravine below to a point just
upstream of the sanctuary in the valley.

From the beach and bay of Xeropotamos below, a
track leads back up the valley into the interior. Following this track for about 700m and then striking up right
towards the top of (the first shoulder of) the hill to the
south west of the site, you come, at the summit, to the
scant remains of a **Venetian fortification**, probably of
the 16th century—the base of a stone tower (about 5
x 10m) in rough masonry, bound in an improvised ce-
ment. In front (towards the northeast) are the founda-

tions of some outer walls, constructed on the plan of a half-octagon.

All over these hills grows a species of **dwarf wild cedar**. These small plants have long lives, during the course of which their trunks and branches are sculpted and twisted by the winds into beautiful and improbable shapes. The wood is very hard and resistant, and is used for short rafters to support the stone roofs of the older houses on the island.

The interior of the island is easy to see on foot, and there are good views at all points. About 1.5km south of Potamos, just before the community of Aleviziànà, are three ruined windmills on the ridge just beside the road: a little beyond this, above the road to the right, is the **Antikythera Bird Observatory of the Hellenic Ornithological Society** (www.ornithologiki.gr), housed in what used to be the primary school building of Aleviziànà. This recently established study-centre is dedicated to the documentation and observation of the massive bird migrations which pass across the island in spring and autumn: the society organises the ringing of migratory birds, who use the island as a stop-over on their route north or south. Even outside of the migration seasons, the whole island seems particularly full of bird-life—flycatchers, songbirds of all kinds, raptors, and, most interesting of all, the **Eleonora's falcon**.

ELEONORA'S FALCON

Falco eleonorae, or the Black Peregrine Falcon, breeds predominantly in the Greek Islands and winters mainly in Madagascar. Around three quarters (approaching 3,000 pairs) of the total population of the species nest in Greece and its islands, and the single largest colony in the world is on Antikythera. Eleonora's falcon is unusual for a raptor in as much as it breeds, not solitarily, but in colonies. The restriction of its breeding area to very few marine geographical localities has probably evolved to take advantage of a concentrated and predictable seasonal food-resource—namely the quantities of migrating songbirds. The falcon breeds unusually late, with the young hatching towards the end of August, thus permitting the newly flying juveniles to take advantage of the prey presented by the autumn migrations. At other times of year, and in its wintering in Madagascar, it customarily lives off large moths and insects, changing its diet only for the migratory season. The fact that such a particular evolutionary pattern should have occurred gives some idea of how long these islands must have been important staging-posts for smaller birds in migration.

The concentration of collective breeding populations in such a small area brings with it problems however: it makes the raptors more vulnerable to disturbance and eventual predation by humans, as well as by the animals that humans often inadvertently introduce—especially rats. For this reason, the special protection afforded on Antikythera and on other Aegean islands, is of the greatest importance in maintaining stable populations of the falcon.

Seen against the sky its silhouette can easily be confused with that of the Peregrine falcon, although its profile is slimmer and its wings and tail longer than the Peregrine. Both the tail and the chestnut underside are conspicuously and elegantly barred. It is superb and playful in flight, recognisable by its repeated staccato call and conspicuous by its unusually gregarious behaviour.

The road ends at **Galanianà**, where the church of the island's patron saint, Aghios Myron, is situated in the fold of a valley, with a simple graveyard under the shade of dense almond trees, and with a wide, rather neglected courtyard in front. The 19th century iconostasis inside the church has an unusual depiction of *Christ as the True Vine* with the Apostles attached like clusters of grapes. Across the valley on the hillside opposite are deserted communities, their buildings now in ruins; further back down the road from Galanianà are some substantial houses in better condition and in a simple local architectural style. Some have finely constructed and sizeable wells, with stone surmounts and overflows.

At the junction below Galanianà, a road signposted to Katsanevianà first drops into the valley and then climbs up to a saddle below the craggy ridge of Mount Prophitis Elias; to the left of the road on the hillside is another deserted settlement with windmill above. Over the saddle, the road now descends into a landscape that is quite different—a wide, sloping, open plateau looking towards the looming and magnificent mountains of western Crete. The earliest Minoan colonists who came to Antikythera must surely have wanted to settle here in sight of the mother island: but they may have encountered a two-fold problem—a lack of water and an absence of safe anchorage along the eastern shore.

There are two 'communities' on the plateau, each consisting today of one (year-round) unit of habitation: Tsikaliarianà to the east, and Katsanevianà to the south.

In a field between the two is the church of Aghios Giorgios. This is a small simple rural chapel: perhaps because
of its palpable remoteness it is all the more surprising and
rewarding to find in its interior a beautiful 17th century
icon of St George, which stands out clearly from all the
others.

Beyond Katsanevianà, a path leads a further 2.5km to
the southern extremity of the island and to the **Apolitara lighthouse**, constructed in un-dressed, local stone in
1926. The walk gives ample opportunity to appreciate the
island's human solitude, yet teeming bird life.

PRACTICAL INFORMATION

801 00 **Antikýthera:** area 19sq.km; perimeter 32km; resident population 39; max. altitude 378 m. **Port Authority:** 27360 33767. **Information:** www.antikythira.gr (website currently under construction). **Travel information:** Porfyra Travel, Kythera, T. 27360 31888.

ACCESS

Access is only by ferry and from the same ports which serve the island of Kythera (*see above*), i.e. from Neapolis (one weekly (Tuesday) sailing–3.5 hrs: T. 27340 22660/ & 24004); Gytheion (four sailings per week—5.5 hrs: T. 27330 22207); Kalamata (one sailing per week (Sat)–7.5 hrs); and from Kisamos in eastern Crete (five sailings per week–2 hrs: T. 28210 28217 & 24147). One of these last sailings also goes on to make the weekly connection to Piraeus. In winter months services are reduced, and information should be obtained at the time of travelling from the local offices on Kythera or on Crete.

LODGING

There are only a small number of rooms for rent, all in the village of Potamos (the port). These are best arranged by going to the island's (unmarked) shop-cum-post-office (*T. 27360 38143*) just above and to the right of where the boat arrives. By shouting the message abroad, the shop-keeper, Myron Patakakis, will raise the mayor, who—in time—provides a simple room for lodging.

EATING

Antikythera has no taverna as yet; but Mr Patakakis, on request, will provide food on a table in front of his shop. His careful and flavourful salad is made with locally grown vegetables—something increasingly rare in Greece. He also has exceptionally good *wine—strong, pinkish-amber in colour, and slightly salty from the exposure of the grapes to the sea air. Mr Patakakis is a mild-mannered and helpful person; he is the best contact for most practical needs during a stay on the island.

ELAFONISOS

'*Elaphon nisos*' means 'island of deer'. A mediaeval Arabic manuscript also appears to refer to the island as '*Ashab al baqar*', which means the same. The deer are all now gone, together with the dense vegetation which once provided for and protected them. Elafónisos today is thinly inhabited and only partially treed, but it lives on a small but vigorous fishing fleet—and on the fame of its few, very fine sandy beaches which draw people in the summer months from all over Greece. Slowly its population is rising, as holiday-makers fall prey to its enchantment and decide to stay and build a house: it remains to be seen whether this tendency can be kept within the limitations of the capacity and tranquillity of the island.

The island is only 400m from the mainland of the southern Peloponnese, just west of Neapolis in the Gulf of Laconia. In Antiquity it is mentioned by Strabo as a promontory called '*Onou gnathos*' or 'ass's jaw', perhaps from the profile the island presents to the bay. After an earthquake, said to have occurred in 375 AD, it was severed from the mainland and separated in the process from an ancient settlement of considerable importance—the Bronze Age site at Pavlopetri, now on the promontory opposite and partly underwater between the present coast and the islet of Pavlopetri. In the vicinity of the embarkation point for the island at Pounta, towards the northwest, are the remains of ancient sandstone quarries and the base of an interesting pyramidal funerary monument, which was seen by Pausanias. It was also in these protected waters in the lea of the island on 30 September 1827, three weeks before the Battle of Navarino (the last naval battle in maritime history to be fought exclusively with sailing ships), that Admiral (Sir Edward) Codrington met with the French and Russian naval high commands, to discuss a strategy that was in the end to give unstoppable momentum to the movement of Greek Independence.

The port of **Elafónisos** is at the northern extremity of the island. The water that separates it from the mainland is of an unforgettable colour when the wind is still, since the strait is shallow and has sand below: as if in competition, the fishing-boats also seem more colourful here than usual. The town's main church, **Aghios Spyridon**, stands on a promontory to the west side of the harbour. The church was founded in 1852, and later restored in 1880: it has an impressive, ornately carved iconostasis in *poros* stone, with an intricate vine motif incorporating a variety of birds and animals.

Four kilometres down the west coast of the island,

against the foot of the hill to your left on entering the inhabited area of Kato Nisi, are the remains of a **round tower**. The fact that its design is of a kind similar to those found on the mainland in the Mani has led people generally to give the tower a late date; but its masonry more accurately suggests mediaeval construction. The stones in the interior are densely and meticulously packed, and sealed with a deep red mortar, which was prepared with crushed tiles: the tower must have been, for its size, remarkably impregnable and was probably a defensive outpost built by the local landowners to protect the barely cultivable lands of the Kato Nisi valley. At 4.5km the road terminates at the church of the Panaghia, built over the site of an earlier Byzantine church. Approximately 200m to the west of the church, a Mycenaean cemetery with rock-cut tombs has been identified.

The road down the eastern seaboard, leaves Elafónisos by the church of Aghios Ioannis; after 4km it passes to the left (east) the western slope of Frango Hill, on which there are the vestiges of an ancient settlement. Some ancient materials have been re-used for the construction of a more recent (possibly mediaeval) habitation at the north end of the area. The road ends 300m beyond at **Simos**—one of the most beautiful beaches in the whole area—backed by junipers and small cedars, and looking across to the acropolis-like promontory of Cape Elena, with its delicate and picturesque isthmus.

PRACTICAL INFORMATION

230 53 Elafónisos: area 17sq.km; perimeter 29km; resident population 746; max. altitude 276m. **Port Authority**: T. 27340 22228. **Travel and information**: www.elafonisos.net

ACCESS

Access is by ferry from the embarkation point at Pounta, 9km northwest of Neapolis in the south east corner of the Peloponnese. Ferries leave every 2 hrs, from 8.30–7.30. There are also summer crossings directly from Neapolis.

LODGING

The number of hotels and houses offering rooms and studios increases every year. For comfortable lodging, a good place to start is the **Hotel Elaion** (*mobile T. 697 670.4706, www.elafonisoselaion.gr*); or the **Hotel Elafonisos** (*T. 27340 61268, fax 61189, www.hotelelafonisos.gr*)

GLOSSARY OF CLASSICAL & BYZANTINE TERMS

amphora—a tall, terracotta receptacle with handles for the transportation of liquids

apotropaic—having the power to turn away evil

Archaic period—the 7th and 6th centuries BC

catholicon—the church at the centre of an Orthodox monastery

deësis—a pictorial composition in Byzantine art which became current after the 11th century, in which the figure of Christ is flanked by interceding Saints, most commonly Mary and St John the Baptist

dentils—the cut, rectangular, teeth-like decorations on the underside of a cornice

Dioscouri—Castor and Polydeuces, twin sons of Zeus; saviours and protectors of mariners

exedra—an architectural protrusion or a free-standing structure of semicircular form

'**free cruciform plan**' – design of a church in which the lateral arms protrude freely from the body of the building (cp. 'inscribed cross plan' below)

Geometric period—the 10th–late 8th centuries BC

Hellenistic period—era of, and after, the campaigns of

Alexander the Great, c. 330–c. 150 BC

iconostasis—the high wooden screen (generally holding icons and images) which separates the sanctuary from the main body of an Orthodox church, and which with time came to substitute the masonry *templon* (*see below*) of earlier Byzantine churches

'**inscribed cross plan**' or 'cross-in-square'—design of a church whose exterior is square, but within which the interior space is articulated in the shape of a cross

isodomic—(of masonry) constructed in parallel courses of neatly-cut rectangular blocks

loculi—compartments, or excavated rectangular tombs, for burial

naos—the central interior area of a Byzantine church or the inside chamber of a pagan temple

narthex—the entrance vestibule of a Byzantine church, often running the width of the building

nymphaeum—a place (often by a spring or in a grotto or underground) consecrated to the worship of the nymphs— divinites of springs and fresh water

oculus—(in architecture) a circular aperture for letting in light from above

poros stone—any soft limestone of porous composition used for construction

pronaos—the front vestibule of a temple, preceding the *naos*

squinch—the solid triangles between the four arches that support the rim on which a dome is to be raised; squinches are simpler than pendentives and can sometimes take the form of corner arches or niches

stade or *stadion*—an ancient Greek measurement of distance equivalent to c. 600ft or 180m

synthronon—the rising, concentric rings of seats for the clergy in the apse of a church

templon—a stone or masonry screen in a church which closes off the sanctuary

tesserae—the small pieces of coloured stone or glass-paste which compose a mosaic

INDEX

Nigel McGilchrist is an art historian who has lived in the Mediterranean—Italy, Greece and Turkey—for over 30 years, working for a period for the Italian Ministry of Arts and then for six years as Director of the Anglo-Italian Institute in Rome. He has taught at the University of Rome, for the University of Massachusetts, and was for seven years Dean of European Studies for a consortium of American universities. He lectures widely in art and archaeology at museums and institutions in Europe and the United States, and lives near Orvieto.